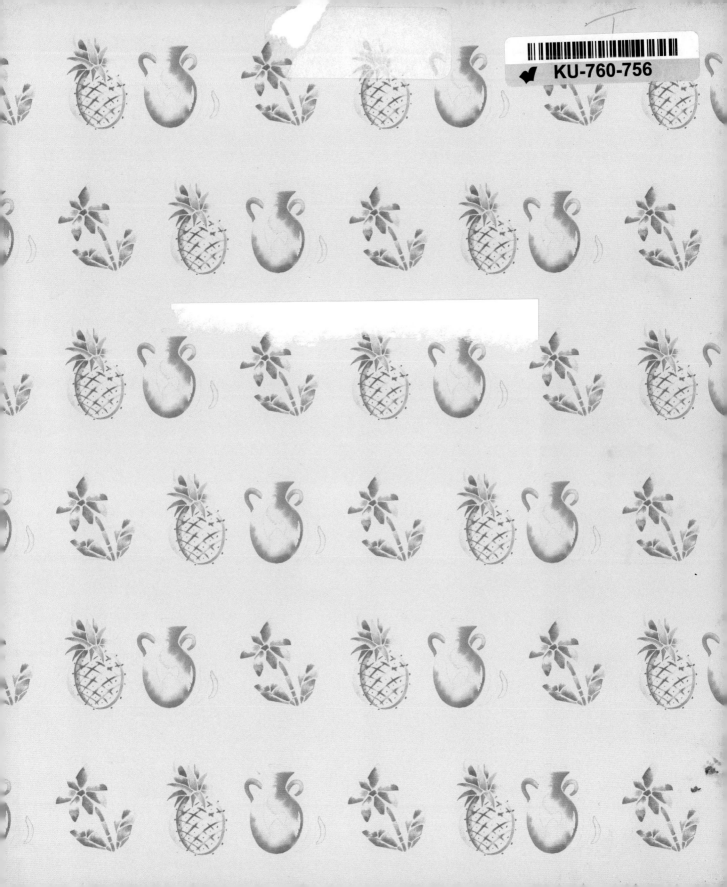
KU-760-756

Complete Paint Effects

Inspirational projects for decorating your home with flair and style

Complete Paint Effects

Inspirational projects for decorating your home with flair and style

SACHA COHEN AND MAGGIE PHILO

PHOTOGRAPHY BY LIZZIE ORME AND ADRIAN TAYLOR

LORENZ BOOKS

HIGHLAND
LIBRARIES

99 35074

747.3

First published in 1999 by Lorenz Books

© Anness Publishing Limited 1999

Lorenz Books is an imprint of
Anness Publishing Limited
Hermes House
88-89 Blackfriars Road
London SE1 8HA

This edition distributed in Canada by
Raincoast Books
8680 Cambie Street
Vancouver
British Columbia V6P 6M9

All rights reserved. No part of this publication may be reproduced, stored in a retrieval system,
or transmitted in any way or by any means, electronic, mechanical, photocopying, recording
or otherwise, without the prior written permission of the copyright holder.

ISBN 1 85967 973 0

A CIP catalogue record for this book is available from the British Library

Publisher: Joanna Lorenz
Senior Editor: Caroline Davison
Project Editors: Clare Nicholson and Lindsay Porter
Production Controller: Don Campaniello
Photographers: Lizzie Orme and Adrian Taylor
Designers: Bobbie Colegate-Smith, Lilian Lindblom and Ian Sandom
Jacket Designer: Lisa Tai
Stylists: Katie Gibbs and Judy Williams
Illustrators: Madeleine David and Lucinda Ganderton

Previously published as three separate volumes in the *Inspirations* series: *Paint Effects*, *Stamping* and *Stencilling*.

Printed and bound in Singapore

1 3 5 7 9 10 8 6 4 2

CONTENTS

INTRODUCTION

Home decorating is not simply a matter of painting your walls with white emulsion; there is a wealth of different paints in amazing colours, and many original, easy ways to apply them, both to walls and to the objects within the room itself. With just a little imagination and a lot of fun you can create originality and colour throughout your home. *Complete Paint Effects* brings together the easiest and

most adaptable of decorative paint techniques, together with fabulous ideas for applying them to the surfaces of your home.

The projects in this book range from the simple to the more complicated, so there is something for every level of expertise and ability. Each project is explained fully with clear step-by-step instruc-

tions and photographs. If you are planning to overhaul a whole room, you will find many ideas for different ways of decorating walls, doors, even floors. Why not create instant lime-washed walls, antique-effect doors, or stunning imitation kitchen tiles? Alternatively, you can use stencils and stamping to add a distinctive pattern of Greek urns, animal friezes, or celestial cherubs to a wall. Decorating smaller objects, such as picture frames, trays, candles and cushions, can also add interest, particularly where there is not much space. These smaller projects are also ideal for giving away as presents.

Each of the main sections on paint effects, stencilling and stamping is preceded by invaluable advice on all the basic techniques for that effect as well as details of the materials and equipment that you will need. There is also clear guidance on mixing your own paint, working with glazes and varnishes, and making your own stencils and stamps.

Armed with this compendium of decorative projects, you will never be short of inspiration for transforming every room of your home with colour and pattern. The only limit is your imagination…

PAINT EFFECTS

Many people find the thought of painting their homes rather daunting, but it is worth bearing in mind that a room can be completely transformed by just a single layer of well-chosen paint. If you use some of the decorative paint effects described in this first section of the book, such as mock 3-D panels, frescoes, crackle glazing, sponging, and graining, the room is guaranteed to look unusual, stylish and highly professional.

   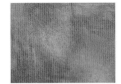

The rooms in many homes are perfectly colour coordinated down to the finest details, from the walls to the floors and from the soft furnishings to the picture frames and other decorative objects. However, you may find yourself getting carried away after looking at the wealth of bright and subtle colours used in the following painting projects and wanting to include as many colours as possible! Today, there is an ever-increasing range of beautiful paints to choose from as well as helpful facilities in many shops for mixing your own paints to create a highly individual scheme.

PAINTING MATERIALS

Acrylic or emulsion (latex) paint and acrylic scumble glaze are the main materials you need to put a wide variety of paint techniques into practice.

ACRYLIC PRIMER is a quick-drying, water-based primer. It can be used to prime new wood.

ACRYLIC SCUMBLE is a slow-drying, water-based medium with a milky, gel-like appearance, which dries clear. It adds texture and translucency to the paint, and the marks you make with brushes, sponges and other tools are held in the glaze.

ACRYLIC VARNISH is available in a satin or matt (flat) finish. It is used to seal paint effects to give a more durable surface. Acrylic floor varnish is hardwearing and should be used on floors.

ARTIST'S ACRYLIC PAINT can be found in art and craft shops. It gives various paint effects a subtle translucent quality.

CRACKLE GLAZE is brushed on to a surface, causing the paint laid over it to crack in random patterns to create an aged appearance.

EMULSION (LATEX) PAINT is opaque and comes in a choice of matt (flat) or satin finish. Satin finish is usually best for the base colour and matt (flat) for paint

effects. Use sample pots of paint if you need only a small amount.

METHYLATED SPIRIT (denatured alcohol) is a solvent that will dissolve emulsion (latex) paint and can be used to distress paint. It is also a solvent, thinner and brush cleaner for shellac.

PURE POWDER PIGMENT can be mixed with acrylic scumble, clear wax or emulsion (latex) paint. It is also used for vinegar graining.

SHELLAC is a type of varnish, available in clear and brown shades. French polish and button polish are in fact shellac and may be easier to find. It can be used to seal wood, metal leaf and paint.

WAX is available in neutral and in brown. It will seal and colour paint. Neutral wax can be mixed with powder pigment.

Opposite: 1 powder pigments, 2 emulsion (latex) paints, 3 acrylic primer, 4 artist's acrylic colours, 5 acrylic scumble, 6 crackle glaze, 7 neutral wax, 8 brown wax, 9 methylated spirit (denatured alcohol), 10 brown shellac, 11 clear shellac.

PAINTING EQUIPMENT

Different paint effects require different tools. Most tools are cheap and easily found in DIY (hardware) or decorating suppliers.

ABRASIVES Sandpaper and wire (steel) wool come in many grades. They are used for distressing paint.

ARTIST'S PAINTBRUSHES are needed to paint fine detail.

DECORATOR'S PAINTBRUSHES are used to apply emulsion (latex) paint, washes and glazes. They come in a wide range of sizes.

FLAT VARNISH BRUSHES can be used for painting and varnishing. They are often the favourite choice of paint effect experts.

MASKING TAPE comes in many types. Easy-mask and low-tack tapes are less likely to pull off paintwork, and flexible tape is good for going around curves. Fine line tape is useful for creating a narrow negative line.

MEASURING EQUIPMENT A ruler, spirit (carpenter's) level, set square (T square) and plumb-line are needed to mark out designs.

MUTTON CLOTH (STOCKINET) is very absorbent and can be used for paint effects. Cotton cloths are also used for ragging and polishing.

NATURAL SPONGES are used for sponging. They are valued for their textural quality. Synthetic sponges can be used for colourwashing.

PAINT KETTLES, trays and pots are used to mix and store paint.

PAINT ROLLERS, small and large, are used for textured effects and to provide an even-textured base colour without brushmarks.

RUBBER COMBS AND HEART GRAINERS (ROCKERS) are used to create textured patterns in paint glazes. Heart grainers (rockers) create an effect of the heart grain of wood.

STENCIL BRUSHES are for stippling paint on to smaller surfaces.

STIPPLING BRUSHES, usually rectangular, are used to even out the texture of glaze and to avoid brushmarks.

Opposite: 1 paint containers, 2 spirit (carpenter's) level, 3 plumbline, 4 kitchen paper (paper towels), 5 artist's brushes, 6 decorator's brushes, 7 flat varnish brushes, 8 hog softening brush, 9 stencil brush, 10 paint rollers, 11 gloves, 12 stippling brush, 13 masking tapes, 14 measuring equipment, 15 craft knife and pencil, 16 heart grainer (rocker), 17 combs, 18 sponges, 19 mutton cloth (stockinet), 20 rag, 21 wire (steel) wool and sandpaper.

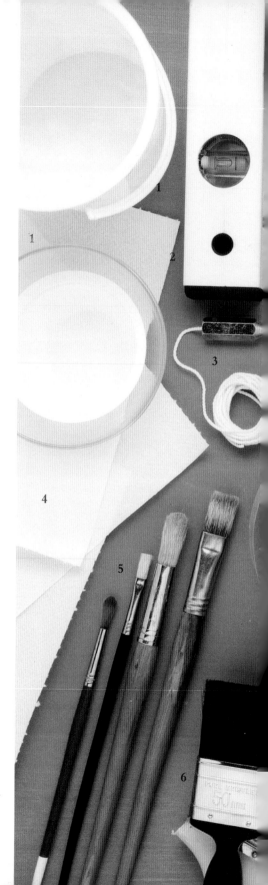

PAINTING TECHNIQUES

Most of the projects in this book are based on a few simple techniques. These can be used on their own, or combined to produce an infinite variety of paint effects.

The techniques shown here all use ultramarine blue emulsion (latex) paint. This has been mixed with acrylic scumble glaze and/or water, as appropriate, to achieve the desired effect. Two coats of silk finish white emulsion (latex) paint were rolled on as a base. This provides an even-textured, non-absorbent finish, which is ideal to work on as it allows glazes to dry more slowly and evenly than emulsion (latex) paint and mistakes are easily wiped off.

All these techniques, except the crackle glaze, can be done with artist's acrylic paint mixed with scumble; then the effects will look more translucent.

SPONGING

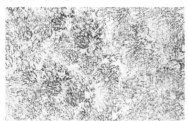

Dilute a little paint with a little water in a paint tray or saucer. Dip a damp, natural sponge into the paint and wipe off the excess on kitchen paper (paper towels). Dab the sponge on to the surface in different directions.

SPONGING AND DISPERSING

Follow the technique as for sponging, then rinse the sponge in clean water and dab it over the sponged paint before it dries to soften the effect.

COMBING

Mix paint with acrylic scumble and brush on with cross-hatched brushstrokes. Run a metal or rubber graining comb through the wet glaze. This pattern was done with straight vertical strokes and wavy horizontal ones.

COLOURWASHING

Dilute the paint with water and brush on randomly with cross-hatched brushstrokes, using a large decorator's brush. A damp sponge will give a similar effect.

RUBBING IN COLOURWASH

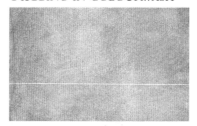

Dilute the paint with water and brush on. Use a clean cotton rag to disperse the paint. Alternatively, apply it directly with the rag and rub in.

FROTTAGE

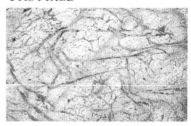

Apply paint with cross-hatched brushstrokes, then press a piece of tissue paper over the wet surface and peel it off. The paint can be diluted with water or scumble.

DABBING WITH A MUTTON CLOTH (STOCKINET)

Brush on paint mixed with scumble, using cross-hatched brushstrokes. Dab a mutton cloth (stockinet) over the wet glaze to even out the texture and eliminate the brushstrokes.

RAGGING

Mix paint with scumble and brush on, using cross-hatched brushstrokes. Scrunch up a piece of cotton rag and dab this in all directions, twisting your hand for a random look. When the rag becomes too paint-soaked, use a new one.

RAG ROLLING WITHOUT BRUSHMARKS

Brush on paint mixed with scumble and dab with a mutton cloth (stockinet) to eliminate brushmarks. Scrunch a cotton rag into a sausage shape and roll over the surface, changing direction as you go. Use a new piece of rag when it becomes too wet.

STIPPLING

Brush on paint mixed with acrylic scumble, using cross-hatched brushstrokes. Pounce a stippling brush over the wet glaze, working from the bottom upwards to eliminate brushmarks and provide an even-textured surface. Keep the brush as dry as possible by regularly wiping the bristles with kitchen paper (paper towels).

DRAGGING

Mix paint with scumble glaze and brush on with cross-hatched brushstrokes. Drag a flat decorator's brush through the wet glaze, keeping a steady hand. The soft effect shown here is achieved by going over the wet glaze again to break up the lines.

CRACKLE GLAZE

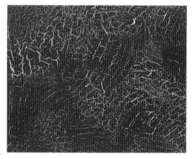

Brush on a coat of water-based crackle glaze and leave to dry according to the manufacturer's instructions. Using a well-laden brush, apply paint carefully on top so that you lay, rather than brush, it over the surface. Work quickly and do not overbrush an area already painted. If you have missed an area, touch it in when the paint has dried. Seal with acrylic varnish.

MIXING PAINTS AND GLAZES

There are no precise recipes for mixing glazes and washes. Generally speaking, the proportion of emulsion (latex) paint to scumble is 1 part paint to 6 parts scumble. This will give soft, semi-translucent colour that is suitable for effects such as ragging, dragging and combing where you want the coloured glaze to hold the marks you have made. If you want a more opaque coverage, you can reduce the amount of scumble, but as the paint will dry more quickly it may be harder to maintain a wet edge for an even result. When you are mixing scumble with artist's acrylic paint, the amount of paint you use depends on the depth of colour you need. Acrylic paint mixed with scumble gives a more translucent colour but it is used in exactly the same way as the emulsion (latex) mix.

If you do not need the texture provided by the scumble (for example, when colourwashing) but you want to dilute the colour, use water. This is cheaper but it dries more quickly, which may be a disadvantage. If you want to slow down the drying time, add a 50/50 mix of water and scumble to the paint. Emulsion (latex) paint can be diluted with any amount of water, and several thin washes of colour will give a more even cover than one thick wash.

Try to mix up enough colour to complete the area you are to decorate. It is difficult to gauge how much you will need. Washes and glazes stretch a long way, but if in doubt, mix up more than you think you might need. If you want to repeat the effect, measure the quantities you use. Before you start, painting samples on to part of the surface or scrap wood will give you the truest effect.

Ragging with acrylic paint and scumble.

Ragging with emulsion (latex) paint and scumble.

Colourwashing with one wash of equal parts emulsion (latex) paint and water.

Colourwashing with four thin washes of 1 part paint to 8 parts water to achieve the same colour saturation.

WORKING WITH COLOUR

Paint effects can vary widely according to your choice of colour and the way in which you use it. Whether you put a light colour over a dark base or a dark colour over a light one is a matter of choice, although a translucent pale colour would not really be visible over a dark base. A bright base colour can give added depth and a subtle glow beneath a dark top coat, while using the colours the other way round will tone down a bright colour. Tone-on-tone colour combinations are good for a subtle effect and are always a safe bet, but experiment with contrasting colours for exciting results.

Many of the techniques in this section use layers of several different colours. Greater depth and texture are achieved when you build up colours in this way, but a simple technique with one colour can be just as effective. It depends on the look you want and the furnishings in the room.

If you want to tone down a paint effect, you can lighten it by brushing over a wash of very diluted white or off-white emulsion (latex) paint. You can also tone down a colour by darkening it. A wash of raw umber paint works well over most colours and has a much warmer feel than black.

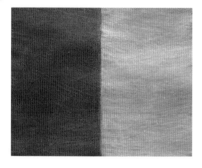

Adding white to lighten bright blue colourwashing.

Adding raw umber to darken bright red colourwashing.

Sponging – light yellow over deep yellow (*left*), deep yellow over light yellow (*right*).

Dabbing with a mutton cloth (stockinet) – dull green over emerald green (*left*), emerald green over dull green (*right*).

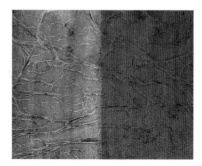

Frottage – tone-on-tone, deep blue over light blue (*left*), tone on contrast, bright blue over orange (*right*).

Colourwashing (*left*) in orange, red and crimson, finishing with the darkest colour.
Sponging (*right*) in three shades of blue-green, finishing with the lightest colour.

MIXING COLOURS

Emulsion (latex) paint is available in a huge range of ready-mixed colours. If you use acrylic paint or pure powder pigment you will need to mix your own colours.

Most colours can be mixed from yellow, cyan blue, magenta, black and white, but a basic palette of 14 colours plus black and white will allow you to mix an enormous range of colours. The suggested palette consists of yellow ochre, cadmium yellow, raw sienna, burnt sienna, red ochre, cadmium red, alizarin crimson, ultramarine blue, Prussian blue, cerulean blue, viridian green, oxide of chromium, raw umber and burnt umber. These basic colours are beautiful alone, and many other colours can be made by mixing them.

Some colour combinations are unexpected, and there are no hard-and-fast rules about which colours should or should not be mixed. If you experiment, you will soon develop confidence and a good eye for mixing colour.

YELLOWS AND BROWNS (*right*)
1 Cadmium yellow and white
2 Cadmium yellow
3 Cadmium yellow and viridian green
4 Yellow ochre and white
5 Yellow ochre
6 Raw sienna
7 Burnt sienna
8 Burnt umber
9 Raw umber

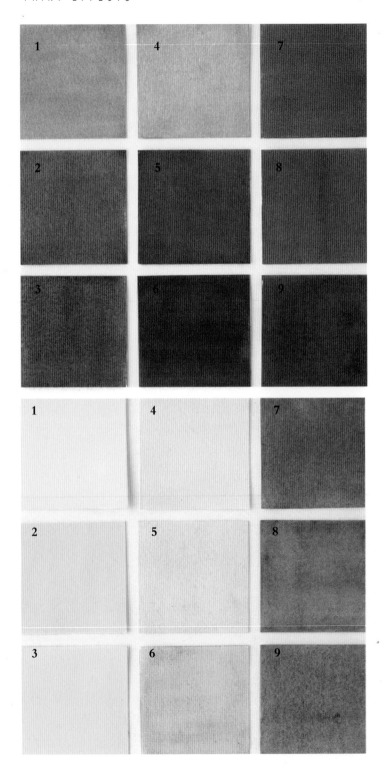

REDS (*opposite*)

1 Alizarin crimson, cadmium yellow and white
2 Cadmium red and cadmium yellow
3 Red ochre
4 Red ochre and white
5 Cadmium red and burnt umber
6 Cadmium red
7 Cadmium red and black
8 Alizarin crimson
9 Alizarin crimson and oxide of chromium

BLUES (*top right*)

1 Cerulean blue, raw umber and white
2 Prussian blue, black and white
3 Prussian blue
4 Cerulean blue
5 Ultramarine blue and white
6 Ultramarine blue
7 Alizarin crimson, ultramarine blue and white
8 Alizarin crimson and ultramarine blue
9 Ultramarine blue and raw umber

GREENS (*right*)

1 Prussian blue, cadmium yellow and white
2 Prussian blue and cadmium yellow
3 Prussian blue and yellow ochre
4 Viridian green and cadmium yellow
5 Oxide of chromium
6 Ultramarine and yellow ochre
7 Prussian blue, yellow ochre and white
8 Viridian green, raw umber and white
9 Viridian green

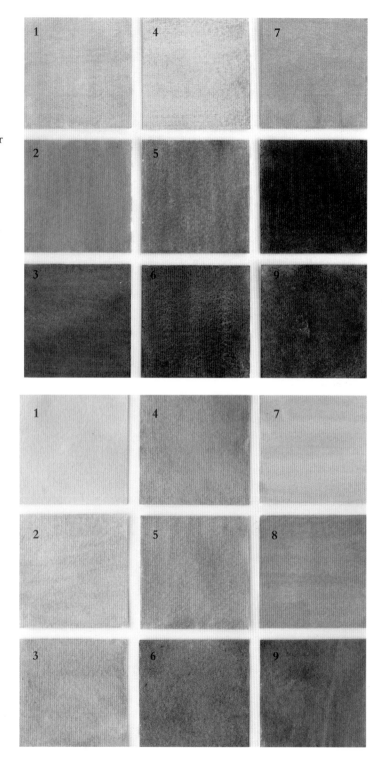

ROUGH PLASTER COLOURWASH

This sunny yellow wall was given a rough-textured look by trowelling on a ready-mixed medium (joint compound), available from DIY (hardware) stores, which is normally used for smoothing walls and ceilings that have unwanted texture. Colourwashing in two shades of yellow gives added depth and tone. The absorbent wall surface picks up varying degrees of paint, and there will be some areas which are not coloured at all, but this is all part of the attractive rural effect.

YOU WILL NEED

medium (joint compound) for coating wall
plasterer's trowel or large scraper
large decorator's paintbrush
white emulsion (latex) paint
bright yellow emulsion (latex) paint, in two
different shades
household sponge

1 Apply the coating medium (joint compound) to the wall, using a plasterer's trowel or large scraper. You can choose to have a very rough effect or a smoother one. Leave to dry overnight.

2 Using a large decorator's paintbrush, paint the wall with two coats of white emulsion (latex), leaving each coat of paint to dry thoroughly.

3 Dilute one shade of yellow paint with about 75% water. Dip a damp sponge into the paint and wipe it over the wall, using plenty of arm movement as though you were cleaning it. Leave to dry.

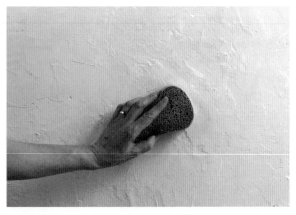

4 Dilute the second shade of yellow paint with about 75% water and wipe it over the first colour in the same way.

DIAMOND-STENCILLED WALL

Here a stunning colour scheme is created by dragging a deep green glaze over a lime green base. The surface is then stencilled with shiny aluminium leaf diamonds, which stand out against the strong background. This paint finish would look very dramatic in a dining room, with muted lighting used just to catch the metallic diamond highlights.

YOU WILL NEED
2 large decorator's paintbrushes
lime green emulsion (latex) paint
monestial green and emerald green artist's acrylic paint
acrylic scumble
pencil
stencil card (cardboard)
craft knife
cutting mat or thick card (cardboard)
2 artist's paintbrushes
acrylic size
aluminium leaf
make-up brush
clear shellac

1 Using a large decorator's brush, paint the wall with lime green emulsion (latex). Leave to dry.

2 Mix a glaze from 1 part monestial green acrylic paint, 1 part emerald green acrylic paint and 6 parts acrylic scumble. Paint the glaze on to the wall with random brushstrokes.

3 Working quickly with a dry brush, go over the surface with long, downward strokes. Overlap the strokes and don't stop mid-stroke. Leave to dry.

▶

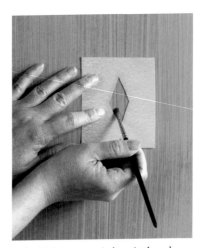

4 Draw a small diamond shape in pencil on to stencil card (cardboard). Cut out, using a craft knife and cutting mat or thick card (cardboard).

5 Using an artist's paintbrush, apply a thin, even coat of acrylic size through the stencil card on to the wall. Repeat as many times as desired to make a decorative pattern.

6 After about 20 minutes, touch the size lightly with a finger to check that it has become tacky. Press a piece of aluminium leaf gently on to the size.

7 Working carefully, peel off the aluminium leaf, then brush off the excess with the make-up brush.

8 Using an artist's paintbrush, apply shellac over the diamond motifs. Leave to dry.

LIMEWASHED WALL

For an instant limewashed effect, apply white emulsion (latex) paint over a darker base with a dry brush, then remove some of the paint with a cloth soaked in methylated spirit (denatured alcohol). This is a good way to decorate uneven or damaged walls.

YOU WILL NEED
cream and white matt emulsion (flat latex) paint
2 large decorator's paintbrushes
old cloths
methylated spirit (denatured alcohol)
neutral wax

1 Paint the wall with a coat of cream emulsion (latex). Leave to dry.

2 Dip the tip of the dry paintbrush into white emulsion (latex). Using random strokes, dry brush the paint on to the wall. Leave to dry.

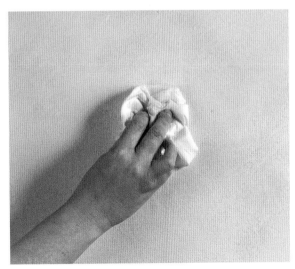

3 Using a cloth, rub methylated spirit (denatured alcohol) into the wall in some areas. Leave to dry.

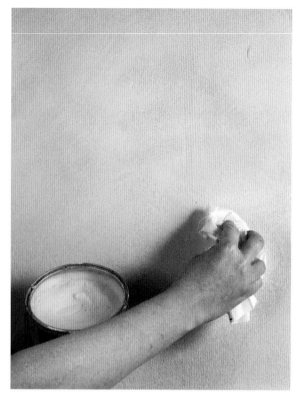

4 Using a clean cloth, rub wax into the wall to seal the paint.

FRESCO EFFECT

A dry brush and cloth are used here to soften rough brushstrokes and give the faded effect of Italian fresco painting. This wall treatment is the ideal background for a mural, so if you are feeling artistic you could paint a scene on top.

YOU WILL NEED
pale pink and ultramarine emulsion
(latex) paint
acrylic scumble
2 large decorator's paintbrushes
old cloth

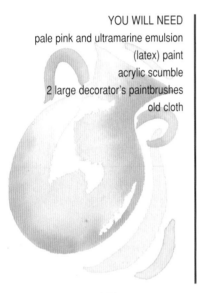

1 Mix a glaze of 1 part pale pink emulsion (latex) to 6 parts acrylic scumble. Paint the glaze on to the top half of the wall with random brushstrokes.

2 Using a dry brush, go over the top half of the wall to even out the brushstrokes.

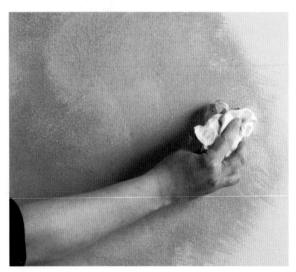

3 Rub a cloth into the glaze with circular motions, to produce the faded effect.

4 Repeat steps 1-3 on the bottom half of the wall, using ultramarine paint. Softly blend the two colours together with a dry brush.

MISTY LILAC STRIPES

Here, wide stripes are painted and the wet paint dabbed with mutton cloth (stockinet) to soften the effect and blend in brushmarks. Careful measuring is required, but it is worth the effort. As an extra touch, paint a triangle at the top of each stripe. If you do not have a picture rail, take the stripes up to the top of the wall and place the triangles along the skirting board (baseboard).

YOU WILL NEED
white silk finish emulsion (latex) paint
paint roller and tray
ruler and pencil
plumbline
masking tape
lilac emulsion (latex) paint
acrylic scumble
medium decorator's paintbrush
mutton cloth (stockinet)
small piece of card (cardboard)
scissors
paint guard or strip of card (cardboard)

1 Paint the walls white, using a paint roller and tray. Mark the centre of the most important wall, below the picture rail (if you have one), with a pencil. Make marks 7.5 cm/3 in either side of this, then every 15 cm/6 in. Continue around the room until the marks meet at the least noticeable corner.

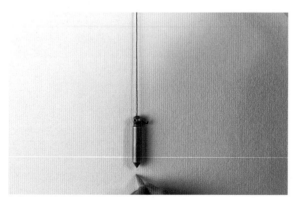

2 Hang a short length of plumbline from one of the marks, and mark with a dot where it rests. Hang the plumbline from this dot and mark where it rests. Continue down the wall. Repeat for each mark below the picture rail.

3 Starting in the centre of the wall, place strips of masking tape either side of the marked row of dots to give a 15 cm/6 in wide stripe. Repeat for the other rows of dots.

4 Dilute some of the lilac paint with about 25% water and 25% acrylic scumble. Brush on to a section of the first stripe. Complete each stripe in two or three stages, depending on the height of the room, blending the joins to get an even result.

5 Dab the wet paint lightly with a mutton cloth (stockinet) to smooth out the brushmarks. Complete all the stripes, then carefully peel away the masking tape and leave the paint to dry.

6 Cut a card (cardboard) triangle with a 15 cm/ 6 in base and measuring 10 cm/4 in from the base to the tip. Use this as a template to mark the centre of each of the stripes, lilac and white, 10 cm/ 4 in below the picture rail.

7 Working on one stripe at a time, place strips of masking tape between the top corners of the stripe and the marked dot, as shown.

8 Brush on the lilac paint mix, then dab the mutton cloth over the wet paint as before. Leave the paint to dry. Repeat for all the stripes.

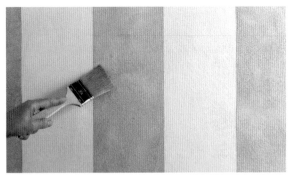

9 Dilute some lilac paint with about 20 parts water. Brush over the wall in all directions to give a hint of colour to the white stripes.

10 Add a little paint to the remaining diluted mixture to strengthen the colour. Using a paint guard or strip of card (cardboard) to protect the painted wall, brush the paint on to the picture rail.

RED-PANELLED WALL

This bright red wall has been beautifully toned down with a translucent glaze of deep maroon acrylic paint mixed with scumble. The panel has been given a very simple trompe l'oeil treatment, using dark and light shades of paint to create a 3-D effect.

YOU WILL NEED
bright red silk finish emulsion (satin finish latex) paint
small and medium decorator's paintbrushes
ruler and pencil
spirit (carpenter's) level
plumbline
masking tape
craft knife
deep maroon, black and white artist's acrylic paint
acrylic scumble
mutton cloth (stockinet)
clean cotton rag
coarse-grade sandpaper

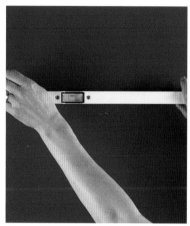

1 Paint the wall with two coats of red paint, leaving each to dry. Mark the centre top of the panel. Draw a horizontal line 30 cm/12 in either side of this mark.

2 Drop a line 90 cm/36 in down from each end of the drawn line and make a mark. Draw a line between all points to give a 60 x 90 cm/24 x 36 in panel.

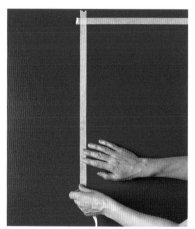

3 Place strips of masking tape around the panel. Neaten the corners with a craft knife.

4 Mix the maroon paint with acrylic scumble to the required colour. Brush this on to the panel.

5 Immediately dab a mutton cloth (stockinet) over the wet paint to even out the texture. ▶

6 Leave the paint to dry. Then, starting in a corner, brush the maroon glaze on to a section of the wall, roughly the same size as the panel. Dab it with the mutton cloth to blend the brushmarks as before, stopping just short of the edge of the panel. Roll up the cotton cloth into a sausage shape and then immediately roll it over the wet glaze, changing direction to give a more random effect. Leave to dry. Repeat with the rest of the wall.

7 Remove the masking tape. Place new strips of tape either side of the bright red line now revealed and trim. Mix a small amount of black acrylic paint with some of the maroon glaze. Brush this between the masking tape down one side of the panel, on the side where the light source is. Place a piece of coarse sandpaper diagonally at the top and clean off the glaze that extends beyond. Keeping the sandpaper in the same position, repeat on the top border of the panel.

8 Add a small amount of white acrylic paint to the maroon glaze and apply to the remaining two borders in the same way. Leave to dry, then carefully remove the masking tape.

TWO-TONE ROLLERED WALL

For this quick, ingenious paint effect, two shades of emulsion (latex) are placed next to each other in a paint tray and then rollered on to the wall together. Moving the roller in different directions blends the paint very effectively.

YOU WILL NEED
paint roller and tray
cream, yellow and terracotta emulsion
(latex) paint

1 Paint the wall with a base coat of cream emulsion (latex), and leave to dry.

2 Pour the yellow and the terracotta emulsion (latex) into the paint tray together, half on each side. The two colours will sit side by side without mixing.

3 Paint the wall, applying the roller at a variety of different angles.

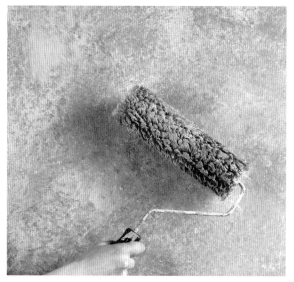

4 When complete, roller over the wall a few times to blend the paint, but don't overwork. ▶

Above: Alternative colours – yellow and cream emulsion (latex) over a dark turquoise base coat.

Above: Complementary colours – light and mid-blue emulsion (latex) over a pale green base coat.

STONE WALL

A subtle stone effect is created using several different techniques. Layers of paint are built up by stippling, sponging and rubbing colours on and off, and a hog softening brush is used to blend the wet glazes to look like stone. The wall is divided by a trompe l'oeil dado (chair) rail.

YOU WILL NEED
large decorator's paintbrush
cream emulsion (latex) paint
spirit (carpenter's) level
ruler
pencil
masking tape
acrylic paint in raw umber, white and yellow ochre
acrylic scumble
decorator's block brush or stippling brush
natural sponge
hog softening brush
old cloths
fine artist's paintbrush

1 Using a large decorator's paintbrush, paint the wall with cream emulsion (latex). Leave to dry.

2 Using a level and ruler, draw pencil lines 6.5 cm/2½ in apart at dado (chair) rail height.

3 Place masking tape inside the two pencil lines, smoothing it in place with your fingers.

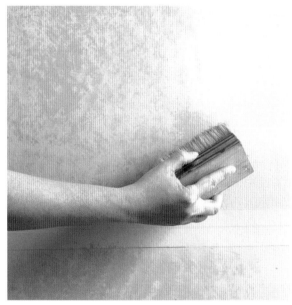

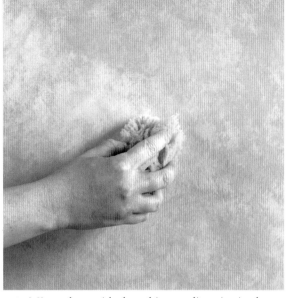

4 Mix a glaze of 1 part raw umber acrylic paint to 6 parts scumble. Stipple this on to the wall, using the tip of the block brush or stippling brush. Avoid the masked area. Leave to dry.

5 Mix a glaze with the white acrylic paint in the same way. Dampen a sponge and apply the glaze over the stippling, varying your hand position to avoid a uniform effect.

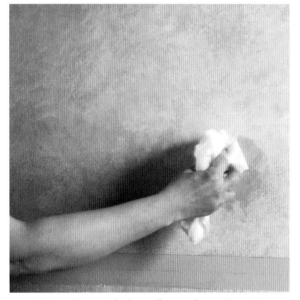

6 Using a hog softening brush, skim gently over the white glaze while it is still wet.

7 Mix a glaze with the yellow ochre paint as in step 4, but this time rub it into the wall with a cloth. Leave some areas of white glaze showing.

8 Using another dampened cloth, rub some areas to disperse the paint. Leave to dry.

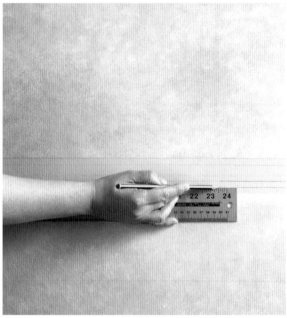

9 Following an illustration or a piece of moulding, draw in the main lines of the false dado rail.

10 Highlight the lines in white acrylic paint, using a fine artist's paintbrush. Leave to dry.

11 Paint the darker areas in raw umber acrylic paint. Leave to dry. Mix in a little white acrylic paint and then add the softer, shadowed areas.

WAX-RESIST SHUTTERS

Give new wooden shutters or doors a weatherworn look by applying wax between two layers of different-coloured paint. Two colourways are shown — creamy yellow beneath bright blue, and pastel blue over candy pink for a sunny, Caribbean feel.

YOU WILL NEED
white acrylic primer
medium and small decorator's paintbrushes
soft yellow and bright blue or candy pink and pale blue matt
emulsion (flat latex) paint
neutral wax
medium-grade sandpaper

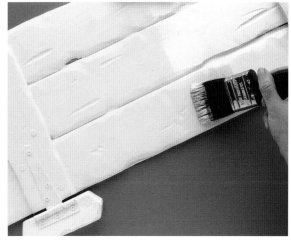

1 Paint the shutters with a coat of white primer and leave to dry. Paint with yellow emulsion (latex). Leave to dry.

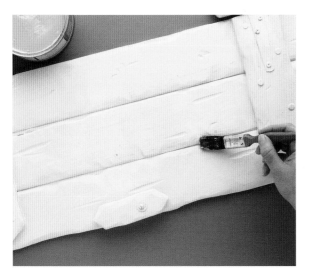

2 Using a small paintbrush, apply wax in areas that would receive wear and tear. Leave to dry.

3 Paint the shutters with blue emulsion (latex). Leave to dry.

4 Sand over the waxed areas to reveal the yellow base colour and create the "worn" effect.

Above: For an alternative colourway, paint candy pink emulsion (latex) over the primer.

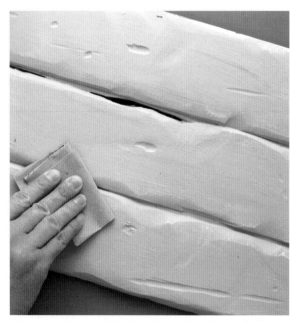

Above: Apply wax as before, then paint with a pale blue top coat. Rub back with sandpaper to reveal areas of pink.

KITCHEN TILES

These clever "tiles" are, in fact, simple squares painted using three different techniques. Fine tape separates the tiles and is removed at the end to give the illusion of grouting.
You can experiment with other paint effects (see Painting Techniques) and colours to create your own design, or leave some of the squares white as a contrast.

YOU WILL NEED
white silk finish emulsion (satin finish latex) paint
standard-size paint roller and tray
ruler and pencil
spirit (carpenter's) level
masking tape
fine line tape or car striping tape
wide easy-mask decorator's tape
ultramarine blue emulsion (latex) paint
small paint roller and tray
natural sponge
kitchen paper (paper towels)
4 cm/1½ in wide decorator's paintbrush
mutton cloth (stockinet)
craft knife (optional)

1 Paint the wall white, using a paint roller for an even texture. Decide on the width of your tiled panel. Mark the wall 45 cm/18 in above your work surface (counter) and in the centre of the width measurement.

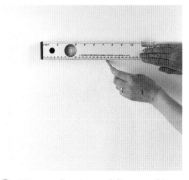

2 Draw a horizontal line at this height, using a spirit (carpenter's) level to make sure that it is straight. Place a strip of masking tape to sit above this line.

3 Mark dots along the tape at 15 cm/6 in intervals either side of the centre mark. Use the spirit level to draw vertical lines down the wall. Mark vertical dots at 15 cm/6 in intervals and draw horizontal lines.

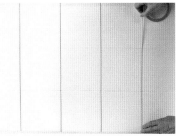

4 Place fine line or car striping tape over the lines in both directions. Smooth the tape into place with your fingers, pressing it down well to ensure that as little paint as possible will be able to seep underneath it.

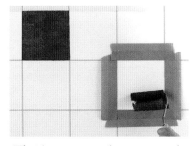

5 Place easy-mask tape around one square. Pour blue paint into the small tray and add 25% water. Apply an even coat of paint to the roller, then roll it over the square. Repeat for all the plain blue squares.

6 Mask off a square to be sponged. Dampen the sponge, dip it into the blue paint and dab the excess on to kitchen paper (paper towels). Sponge the paint on the square. Repeat for all the sponged squares.

7 Mask off a square to be dabbed with the mutton cloth (stockinet). Using a brush, apply the paint and then use the cloth to blend it. Continue as before.

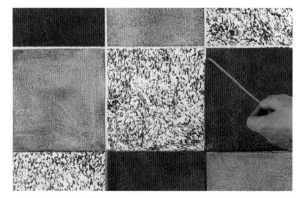

8 Remove all the tape and clean off the pencil marks. If paint has seeped under the tape in places, use a craft knife to scrape it off.

FROTTAGE HALLWAY

The technique of texturing paint by pressing tissue paper over the wet surface is known as "frottage". Here, tone-on-tone in soft shades of green create the delicate effect shown at the top of the hallway. The pattern in the textured wallpaper below the dado (chair) rail has been highlighted by stippling on a darker green glaze, then wiping it off with a cloth to reveal the raised areas.

YOU WILL NEED
light, medium and dark shades of soft green and white silk finish
emulsion (satin finish latex) paint (buy a dark shade and mix it
with white to make the light and medium shades)
large and medium decorator's paintbrushes
medium shade of soft green matt emulsion (flat latex) paint
tissue paper
acrylic scumble
stippling brush
clean cotton rag

1 Paint the upper part of the wall with two coats of light green silk finish paint, leaving each to dry.

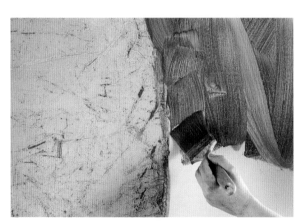

2 Dilute the matt (flat) green paint with about 20% water. Brush this on to a section of the wall.

3 Immediately press a sheet of tissue paper over the entire surface except for a narrow band adjacent to the next section you will be working. Work on a manageable area at a time so that you can keep the edge wet. Better still, ask someone to assist you – one brushing, one following with the tissue paper.

4 Carefully peel back the tissue paper to reveal most of the base colour.

5 Brush on two coats of medium green silk finish paint over the textured wallpaper below the dado (chair) rail, leaving each to dry. If the wallpaper is new, it may bubble, but it will shrink back when dry.

6 Mix dark green silk finish paint with acrylic scumble in a ratio of one part paint to six parts scumble. Brush this glaze on to a section of the wallpaper.

7 Immediately dab over the wet glaze with a stippling brush to eliminate brushmarks and even out the texture.

8 Wipe a cotton cloth gently over the stippled glaze to remove it from the raised areas of the wallpaper. Complete the wall section by section. Paint the dado rail with white paint, leave to dry and then brush over the dark green glaze.

VINEGAR-GLAZED FLOORCLOTH

Painted floorcloths were popular with the early American settlers as cheap, handmade alternatives to carpets. This one is painted with vinegar glaze and decorated with patterns, using a cork and other simple objects as stamps. Dark shellac gives an antique finish.

YOU WILL NEED

heavyweight cotton duck canvas (from artist's suppliers), 7.5 cm/3 in larger all round than the finished floorcloth
staple gun or hammer and tacks
white acrylic wood primer
large and medium decorator's paintbrushes
fine-grade sandpaper
set square (T square)
pencil
large scissors
PVA (white) glue and brush
2.5 cm/1 in masking tape
dessertspoon
bright red emulsion (latex) paint
gloss acrylic floor varnish and brush – use matt (flat) acrylic varnish if preferred
1 cm/½ in masking tape
malt vinegar
sugar
bowl and spoon
dark ultramarine powder pigment
reusable tacky adhesive
old cloth
cork
craft knife
dark shellac
floor varnish

PREPARATION

Stretch the canvas across an old door or tabletop and staple or tack in place. Paint with three or four coats of primer, leaving to dry between coats, then sand to give a smooth surface. Using a set square (T square), check that the canvas is square and trim if not. Mark a pencil border 2.5 cm/1 in from the edge. Cut diagonally across each corner, through the point where the pencil lines cross.

1 Fold over each edge to the pencil line. Glue and then secure with masking tape until dry. Rub the edges firmly with a dessertspoon. Sand the edges where the primer has cracked.

2 Turn the canvas to the right side. Using masking tape, mark a wide border. Paint with bright red emulsion (latex), carrying the paint over the outer edges. When dry, apply a coat of floor varnish. Leave to dry.

3 Remove the masking tape and tidy any ragged edges with extra paint. When dry, place 1 cm/½ in masking tape around the outer edge to a depth of 1 cm/½ in. Repeat around the inner edge of the border. ▶

4 Mix 150 ml/¼ pint/⅝ cup malt vinegar with 1 teaspoon sugar. Add up to 2 tablespoons of dark ultramarine pigment and stir well – the glaze should flow on smoothly. Paint the glaze over the red border.

5 While the ultramarine glaze is still wet, make patterns by pressing the reusable tacky adhesive on top and then removing it.

6 Copy the patterns shown or experiment with your own. Wipe the glaze with a damp cloth if you make a mistake. The glaze will take about 15 minutes to dry.

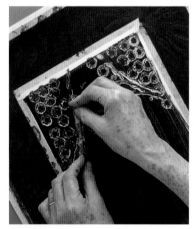

7 Using a craft knife, cut a hole in one end of the cork. Paint the glaze over the centre panel. While still wet, stamp a pattern of circles and lines.

8 Cut a square at the other end of the cork to make a different stamp. Experiment with other objects. Use the reusable tacky adhesive to make additional lines and curves.

9 When dry, remove the masking tape. Tidy the edges with a damp cloth wound around your finger. Apply a coat of dark shellac, then several coats of floor varnish, allowing the canvas to dry between coats. Leave for at least 4 days before using.

COMBED CHECK FLOOR

A simple combing technique has been used to decorate this warm, sunny floor. You can experiment with other patterns instead of the traditional wave pattern shown here. Using a hardboard template to draw the squares saves the chore of measuring and marking out the floor before you start.

YOU WILL NEED
yellow ochre, orange and red emulsion (latex) paint
medium decorator's paintbrush
30 cm/12 in wide piece of hardboard
pencil
masking tape
acrylic scumble
rubber comb
acrylic floor varnish and brush

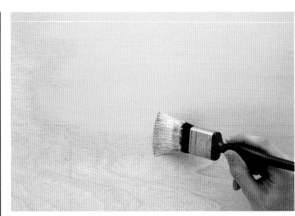

1 Paint the floor with two coats of yellow ochre emulsion (latex), leaving each to dry.

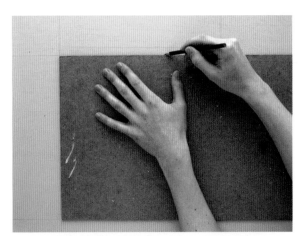

2 Starting in the corner most on view, place the piece of hardboard against the side of the wall. Draw pencil lines widthways across the room. Return to the same corner and draw lines lengthways to form a grid.

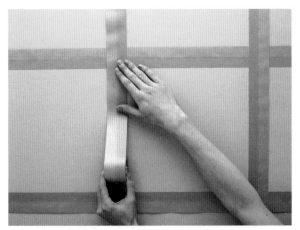

3 Place masking tape on the outside of alternate lines, both horizontally and vertically.

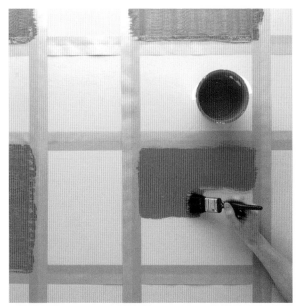

4 Mix some scumble into the orange emulsion (latex). Paint this mixture on to one square (you will need to work on one at a time so that the paint remains wet).

5 Run the comb through the paint, twisting your hand slightly to form a wave pattern. Repeat the process with the orange squares on alternate rows. Leave to dry, then remove the masking tape.

6 Place masking tape the other side of those squares previously marked. Paint these, one at a time, with red emulsion (latex) mixed with scumble.

7 Run the comb through the wet paint, this time in the opposite direction. Half the squares on the floor will now be painted.

8 To complete the remaining squares, simply mask each square individually and then paint in the appropriate colour.

9 Comb each of the squares as you go, while the paint is still wet.

10 When the paint is dry, seal the floor with three coats of acrylic floor varnish.

DISTRESSED TABLETOP

A junkshop buy can be transformed with a fashionably distressed look in shades of blue paint. Petroleum jelly and candle wax resist the paint in different ways. The petroleum jelly is applied to the tabletop in the main areas of natural wear and tear; the candle wax is then used along the edges of the tabletop, giving a more subtle effect.

YOU WILL NEED
sanding block and medium-grade sandpaper
navy blue, pale blue and mid-blue emulsion (latex) paint
small decorator's paintbrush
petroleum jelly and brush
old cloth
candle
matt (flat) acrylic varnish and brush

1 Sand the tabletop to provide a key for the paint.

2 Paint with the navy blue emulsion (latex). Leave to dry.

3 Brush on blobs of petroleum jelly, working inwards from the edges of the table.

4 Paint with pale blue emulsion (latex), applying the brushstrokes in the same direction – don't cover the surface completely. Leave to dry.

5 Wipe over with a cloth and soapy water. In the areas where the petroleum jelly has been applied, the pale blue paint will come away, revealing the navy blue base coat.

6 Rub over the surface of the table with candle wax, concentrating on the edges.

7 Paint the table with mid-blue emulsion (latex), again applying the brushstrokes in the same direction. Leave to dry.

8 Rub over the surface with sandpaper. Where the candle wax has been applied, the mid-blue paint will be removed. Seal with two coats of varnish.

DRY-BRUSHED CHAIR

A soft, distressed look is achieved by dry brushing off-white paint over a light brown base painted to imitate wood. This is another excellent technique for making a tired old piece of furniture look desirably aged.

YOU WILL NEED
old cloth
sanding block and medium-grade sandpaper
pale terracotta and off-white emulsion (latex) paint
small decorator's paintbrush
sponge
matt (flat) acrylic varnish and brush

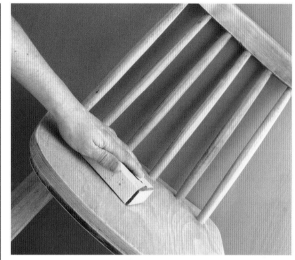

1 Wipe over the chair with a damp cloth, then sand it in the direction of the grain.

2 Mix the pale terracotta emulsion (latex) 50/50 with water. Paint the chair.

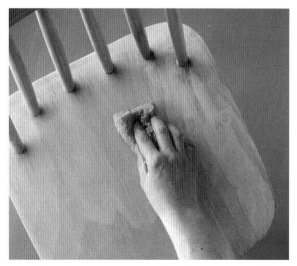

3 Using a sponge dampened with water, carefully remove the excess paint mixture.

63

4 Using a dry brush, apply the off-white emulsion (latex) over the chair. At the angles, flick the paint from the base upwards.

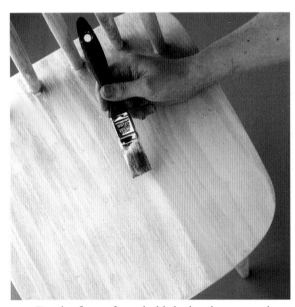

5 For the flat surfaces, hold the brush at an angle and apply the paint with minimal pressure. Seal with two coats of varnish.

GRAINED DOOR

This strongly textured combed graining is achieved by mixing wall filler with sky blue emulsion (latex). Lime green paint is then brushed over the blue and sanded off when dry to give a surprisingly subtle effect.

YOU WILL NEED
medium-grade sandpaper
sky blue and lime green emulsion
(latex) paint
medium decorator's paintbrush
wall filler
rubber comb
matt (flat) acrylic varnish and brush

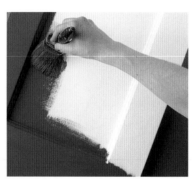

1 Sand the door and then paint it with a base coat of sky blue emulsion (latex). Leave to dry.

2 Mix 25% filler with 75% sky blue emulsion (latex). Paint on to the door, working on one small section at a time. While still wet, comb in lines, following the grain. Leave to dry.

3 Paint the door with a thin coat of lime green emulsion (latex), applying the paint in the same direction as the combing. Leave to dry.

4 Sand the door, revealing lines of blue paint beneath the lime green top coat. Seal with two coats of acrylic varnish.

HARLEQUIN SCREEN

Two simple paint techniques – stippling and rag rolling – are used here to great effect. Choose bright shades of paint as the colours will be softened by the white-tinted scumble glaze.

YOU WILL NEED

three-panel screen with curved top
screwdriver
cream emulsion (latex) paint
medium decorator's brush
fine-grade sandpaper
1 cm/½ in wide masking tape
1 cm/½ in wide flexible masking tape
long ruler or straight piece of wood
water-soluble marker pencil
fine line tape or car striping tape
wide easy-mask decorator's tape
stencil brush
kitchen paper (paper towels)
white palette or old white plate
emulsion (latex) paint in turquoise, red, yellow and green
matt (flat) varnish and brush
white acrylic paint
acrylic scumble
cotton cloth
gold acrylic paint
gold gouache paint
small stencil brush

PREPARATION

It is best to remove the hinges before sanding the surfaces to be decorated. Apply cream emulsion (latex) and leave to dry, then sand to give a smooth surface. Refer to the artworks at the back of the book for templates of how to mark up the screen.

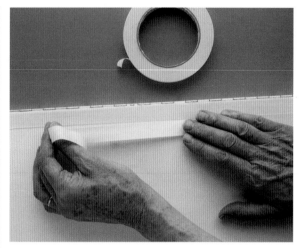

1 Place masking tape close to the edge of the screen along the outer borders of the two outer panels, and along the base of all three panels. Place a second line of tape next to the first.

2 Remove the outer tape, leaving a 1 cm/½ in border along the edge of the screen. Smooth down the remaining tape. Using flexible masking tape, repeat steps 1 and 2 along the top of all three panels.

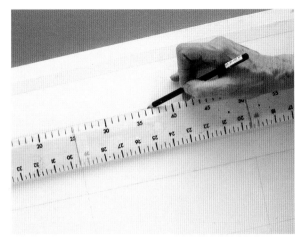

3 Measure the height of the screen at the longest point and divide by six. Draw a vertical line halfway across the panel. Mark the centre point and two equally spaced points either side. Return to the centre point and divide the panel horizontally into four equal points, one each side of the central line. Draw a grid of equal-sized oblongs, four across and six down. Repeat for the other panels.

4 Lay fine line tape or car striping tape from the centre point at the top of each panel diagonally to the far right-hand corner of the next space. Continue from the far right-hand corner through the centre point until all the lines are marked with tape. Repeat in the opposite direction to make a diamond pattern. Secure the tape at the sides of the panel with a small piece of masking tape.

5 Using the wide easy-mask decorator's tape, mask off the diamonds that are to be painted in the first colour. Follow the picture of the finished screen for colour reference.

6 Bind 2.5 cm/1 in at the base of the stencil brush with masking tape. Dip the brush into the first colour, wipe the surplus on kitchen paper (paper towels) until the brush is fairly dry, then stipple the masked diamonds. Work out to the masking tape, using a firm pouncing motion. Leave to dry. Using the other colours, stipple all the diamonds. ▶

7 When all the paint is dry, remove the fine line tape. Apply a coat of matt (flat) varnish and leave to dry. Mix a little white acrylic paint into the scumble to make a glaze. Paint this over the diamonds.

8 Holding a crumpled cloth between both hands, roll it down each panel while the glaze is still wet, moving your hands in different directions. Leave the glaze to dry.

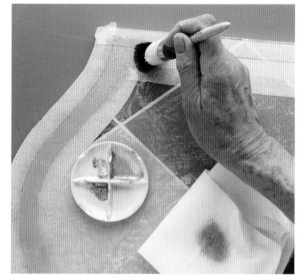

9 Apply another coat of varnish. When this is dry, remove the masking tape from the borders of the diamonds.

10 Mix both gold paints together. Lay masking tape either side of the cream borders. Stipple the gold paint on with a small stencil brush. Leave to dry, then remove the tape. Apply a final coat of varnish. When dry, replace the screen hinges.

GRAINED WINDOW FRAME

Here, extra interest is added to a window frame by decorating it with a subtle imitation wood pattern. The same treatment would work well on a wide picture frame. To hide a boring view, stencil the bottom panes of glass with frosted stars.

YOU WILL NEED
medium- and coarse-grade sandpaper
pale blue-green vinyl silk paint
medium decorator's paintbrush
deep blue-green matt emulsion
(flat latex) paint
water-based scumble
heart grainer (rocker)
old cloth
gloss acrylic varnish and brush
rubber comb
star stencil
masking tape
stencil brush
acrylic frosting varnish

1 Sand the window frame with medium-grade sandpaper, then paint with pale blue-green vinyl silk paint and leave to dry. For the glaze, mix 1 part deep blue-green emulsion (latex) to 6 parts scumble. Paint the glaze over the main surfaces.

2 While the glaze is wet, draw the heart grainer (rocker) across the glazed surface, rocking it backwards and forwards. Wipe the corners with a damp cloth to make a mitre. As you work, protect the wet graining with a piece of sandpaper. Leave to dry.

3 Apply a coat of varnish only over the glazed areas and leave to dry. Paint the inner edges of the frame and the glazing bars across the window with glaze. While still wet, draw down each piece of wood with the rubber comb. Leave to dry, then apply another coat of varnish over the whole window frame.

4 Make sure that the glass is clean, and then attach the stencil with masking tape. Using a stencil brush, apply the frosting evenly through the stencil. Remove the stencil before the varnish dries completely.

CRACKLE-GLAZE PICTURE FRAME

This simple picture frame – which could also be used to hold a small mirror – is made from a piece of plywood. Simply cut a square from the centre and edge with beading. As well as being treated with crackle glaze, the brightly coloured paintwork is distressed slightly with sandpaper to give a very attractive finish.

YOU WILL NEED
yellow ochre, turquoise, orange, lime green and bright pink emulsion (latex) paint
medium and small decorator's brushes
acrylic crackle glaze
masking tape
craft knife
flat artist's paintbrush
coarse-grade sandpaper
acrylic varnish and brush

1 Paint the frame with two coats of yellow ochre emulsion (latex), allowing each to dry. Brush on a coat of crackle glaze. Leave to dry according to the manufacturer's instructions.

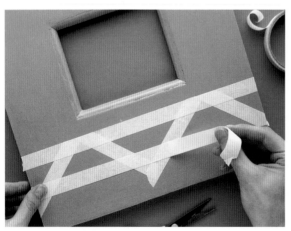

2 Place strips of masking tape in a pattern on either side of the frame, as shown.

3 Where the ends of the tape overlap, carefully trim off the excess with a craft knife.

4 Brush turquoise paint on the unmasked sections of the frame, working in one direction. The crackle effect will appear almost immediately. Take care not to overbrush an area (see Painting Techniques).

5 Brush orange paint on alternate sections of the pattern in the same way. Paint the remaining sections lime green.

6 Leave the paint to dry, and then carefully peel away the masking tape.

7 Using a flat artist's paintbrush, apply bright pink paint to the areas where the masking tape had been. Do this freehand to give the frame a handpainted look. Leave to dry.

8 Rub coarse-grade sandpaper over the crackled paint surface to reveal some of the yellow ochre paint beneath.

9 Seal the frame with two coats of acrylic varnish. Apply the first coat quickly, taking care not to overbrush and reactivate the crackle glaze.

SPONGED LAMP BASE

Three shades of green paint are sponged on to this inexpensive lamp base to give a very attractive dappled surface. If you prefer, you can practise the sponging technique first on a piece of white paper until you are confident. You will quickly discover that it is not at all difficult, despite the very professional-looking result.

YOU WILL NEED
wooden lamp base with flex (electric cord) and light socket
masking tape
scissors
rubber gloves
fine wire (steel) wool
acrylic primer
flat artist's paintbrush
off-white, jade green and emerald green
emulsion (latex) paint
bowl
natural sponge
white paper
clear acrylic varnish and brush

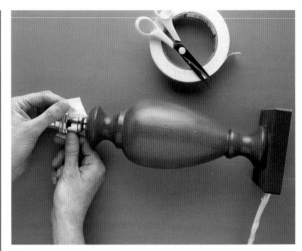

1 Cover the flex (electric cord) and light socket with layers of masking tape to protect them.

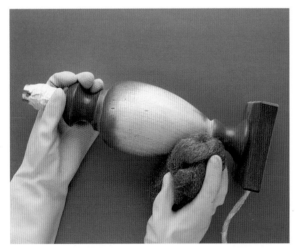

2 Wearing rubber gloves, rub down the existing varnish or paint with wire (steel) wool.

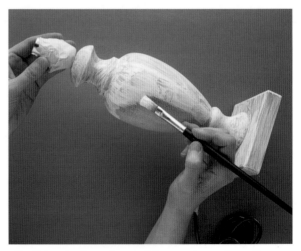

3 Paint the lamp base with two coats of acrylic primer, leaving each to dry.

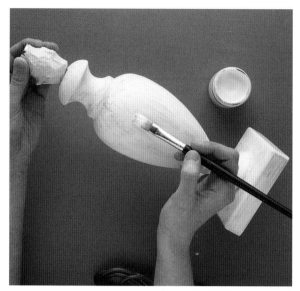

4 Paint with two coats of off-white emulsion (latex), leaving the paint to dry between coats.

5 Mix a 50/50 solution of jade green paint and water. Dampen the sponge and squeeze it until nearly dry, then dip it into the paint. Practise by dabbing the sponge on to a piece of white paper.

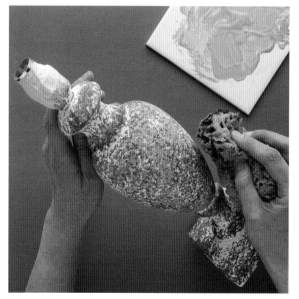

6 Cover the lamp base with a dappled layer of paint, applying it just a little at a time in order to build up the texture gradually.

7 Add some off-white paint to lighten the colour. Sponge this lightly over the first layer of colour. Break off a small piece of sponge and use this to work the colour into the moulding.

8 Mix a little emerald green paint 50/50 with water. Apply this mixture sparingly over the surface of the lamp base to add extra depth and texture. When dry, seal with three coats of varnish, allowing the varnish to dry thoroughly between coats. Finally, remove the protective masking tape from the flex and bulb fitting.

CRACKLE-GLAZE PLANTER

Here, crackle glaze is sandwiched between dark and pale layers of emulsion (latex) paint to give a modern planter an authentic antique look. The handpainted line is easier to do than you might think, and gives a smart finishing touch.

YOU WILL NEED
MDF planter
fine-grade sandpaper (optional)
emulsion (latex) paint in mid-blue and
dark cream
small decorator's paintbrush
acrylic crackle glaze
fine artist's paintbrush
clear acrylic varnish and brush

1 You do not need to prime MDF, but it may need sanding, especially on the cut edges. Paint the inside and outside with mid-blue emulsion (latex).

2 When the paint is completely dry, apply a layer of crackle glaze to the outside of the planter. Leave to dry.

3 Paint the outside of the planter with dark cream emulsion (latex). The crackled effect will start to appear almost immediately, so work as quickly as you can, with regular brushstrokes.

4 Holding your finger against the edge for support, paint a thin mid-blue line 1.5 cm/⅝ in from the edge on each side of the planter. Leave to dry, then seal with two coats of varnish.

82

SCANDINAVIAN TABLE

This pretty little table has been distressed by rubbing back thin layers of colour with fine wire wool. Focusing on the areas that would normally suffer most from general wear and tear gives an authentic aged look. The simple leaf design is painted freehand and picked out with paler highlights. If you are decorating a new wooden table, sand the wood first with fine-grade sandpaper and paint with a coat of primer. Remove the drawer knob.

YOU WILL NEED
MDF or wooden table with drawer
rubber gloves
fine wire (steel) wool
dark yellow, grey-green, white, mid-green and pale
green emulsion (latex) paint
flat artist's paintbrush
small decorator's paintbrushes
acrylic scumble
fine artist's paintbrush
clear matt (flat) acrylic varnish and brush

1 Rub down the table with fine wire (steel) wool, wearing a pair of rubber gloves. Pay particular attention to the bevelled edges.

2 Using dark yellow emulsion (latex), paint the mouldings (if any) around the edge of the drawer and the tabletop.

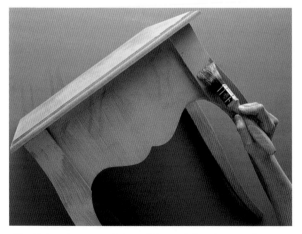

3 Paint the rest of the table and the drawer front with two coats of grey-green emulsion (latex), allowing the paint to dry between coats.

4 Wearing rubber gloves once again, rub down the entire surface with wire wool.

5 Mix 50/50 white emulsion (latex) and scumble. Apply sparsely to the green areas with a dry brush, using light diagonal strokes and varying the angle of the brush to give an even coverage.

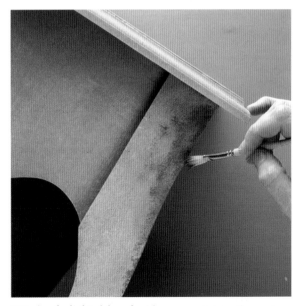

6 Mix 50/50 dark yellow emulsion (latex) and scumble. Paint this over the mouldings.

7 Apply light dabs of mid-green paint to the parts of the table that would receive the most wear: the top corners of the legs and underneath. Leave to dry, then rub back with wire wool.

8 Paint a scrolling leaf design around the edge of the drawer front in pale green. Pick out the stalks and leaf veins with fine brushstrokes in mid-green.

9 Still using the fine artist's paintbrush, add white and yellow highlights to the leaf design.

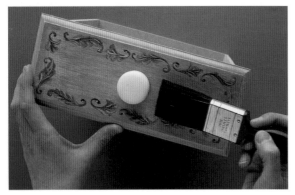

10 Seal the drawer and table with a coat of acrylic varnish for protection.

STENCILLING

Stencilling is very often the first paint effect that people try and it is indeed one of the most enduring and popular of home decorating techniques. Easy to do and relatively inexpensive, it has been used for centuries in interior decoration. Whether you use it boldly in place of wallpaper or simply to add decorative details to walls, furniture and other household objects, you can be sure of achieving an eye-catching effect. You will, in fact, be surprised at how quickly you can transform even a very large surface with a striking pattern.

The joy of stencils is that they can be applied to almost any surface, from fabrics and floors to glass and walls. Although you can buy stencils from DIY (home improvement stores) and other specialist shops, it is much more rewarding and fun to make your own. If you cannot draw your own designs freehand, then there are useful templates at the back of the book for many of the stencils used in these projects. Remember that the colour you use will influence the overall effect. The impact made by using bold bright colours, for example, will be very different from that made by soft subtle hues.

STENCILLING MATERIALS

A variety of materials can be used for stencilling, from specialist stencilling paints and sticks to acrylics and emulsion. Each has its own properties and will create different effects.

ACRYLIC STENCIL PAINTS

Acrylic stencil paint is quick-drying, reducing the chance of the paint running and seaping behind the stencil. Acrylic stencil paints are available in a wide range of colours and can be mixed for more subtle shades.

ACRYLIC VARNISH

This is useful for sealing finished projects.

EMULSION PAINTS

Ordinary household emulsion can also be used for stencilling. It is best to avoid the cheaper varieties as these contain alot of water and will seap through the stencil.

FABRIC PAINTS

These are used in the same way as acrylic stencil paints, and come in an equally wide range of colours. Fixed with an iron according to the manufacturer's instructions, they will withstand washing and everyday use. As with ordinary stencil paint do not overload the brush with colour, as it will seap into the fabric. Always back the fabric you are stencilling with scrap paper or newspaper to prevent the paints from marking the work surface.

GOLD LEAF AND GOLD SIZE

These can be used to spectacular effect. The actual design is stencilled with gold size. The size is then left to become tacky and the gold leaf rubbed over the design.

METALLIC CREAMS

These are available in many different metallic finishes, from gold through to bronze and copper and silver. Apply as highlights on a painted base, or use for the entire design. Creams can be applied with cloths or your fingertip.

OIL-BASED STENCIL STICKS AND CREAMS

The sticks can be used in the same way as a wax crayon, while the creams can be applied with a brush or your fingertip. With either one, there is no danger of overloading the colour, and they won't run. The disadvantage is their long drying time (overnight in some cases); also, the colours can become muddy when mixed. Sticks and creams are also available for fabrics.

Clockwise from top left: acrylic stencil paints, oil-based cream and metallic creams, fabric paints, oil-based stencil sticks, emulsion paints, gold leaf, acrylic varnish and gold size.

STENCILLING EQUIPMENT

Stencilling does not require a great deal of specialist equipment; many of the items used are commonly found in most households. Some items, however, will make the job easier.

BRUSHES
It is worth investing in a set of good stencil brushes. The ends of the brushes should be flat and the bristles firm, to allow you to control the application of paint. A medium-sized brush (1½ in/3 cm diameter) is a useful, all-purpose size, but you may want to buy one size smaller and one size larger as well. You will need a selection of household paintbrushes for applying large areas of background colour, and small artist's paintbrushes for adding fine details.

CRAFT KNIFE OR SCALPEL
Use either for cutting out stencils from card.

CUTTING MAT
This provides a firm surface to cut into and will help prevent the craft knife or scalpel from slipping.

MASKING TAPE
As the stencil may need to be repositioned it is advisable to hold it in place with masking tape, which can be removed fairly easily from most surfaces.

PAINT-MIXING CONTAINER
This may be necessary for mixing paints and colourwashes.

PENCILS
Keep a selection of soft and hard pencils to transfer the stencil design on to card. Use an ordinary pencil to mark the positions of the stencils before applying.

STENCIL CARD
The material used to make the stencil is a matter of preference. Specialty stencil card is available waxed, which means that it will last longer, but ordinary card or heavy paper can also be used. It is worth purchasing a sheet of clear acetate if you wish to keep your stencil design, to reuse time and again.

TAPE MEASURE AND STRAIGHT-EDGES
Some patterns may require accuracy. Measuring and planning the positions of your stencils before you begin will aid the result.

TRACING PAPER
Use to trace and transfer your stencil design on to stencil card.

Clockwise from top left: straight-edges, tape measure, stencil brushes, household paintbrush, cutting mat, stencil card, tracing paper, soft pencil, scalpel, paint-mixing container, masking tape.

STENCILLING TECHNIQUES

Stencilling is not difficult to master, but it is worth practising on a small area to get used to handling the brush and to become accustomed to the properties of the paints you use. Some of the tips and techniques suggested below will make the task easier.

TRANSFERRING TEMPLATES

 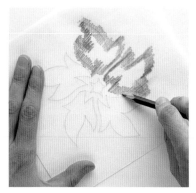 

1 To transfer a template on to a piece of stencil card, place a piece of tracing paper over the design, and draw over it with a hard pencil.

2 Turn over the tracing paper, and on the back of the design rub over the lines you have drawn with a soft pencil.

3 Turn the tracing paper back to the right side and place on top of a sheet of stencil card. Draw over the original lines with a hard pencil.

CUTTING STENCILS

1 Place the stencil on to a cutting mat or piece of thick cardboard and tape in place. Use a craft knife or scalpel for cutting.

2 It is safer to move the cutting board towards you and the knife when working round awkward shapes. Continue, moving the board as necessary.

BLOCK STENCILLING

Use for filling in large areas in a single, solid colour. As in all stencilling, remember not to apply the paint too heavily – less is more. Always blot out the paint on to a piece of blotting card before you begin.

BLOCK STENCILLING WITH SECOND COLOUR STIPPLED

When applying two colours, always apply the lighter shade first, then the darker. Do not cover the entire surface with the first colour; leave a gap for the second shade, then blend later. Use a separate, clean brush for each colour.

TWO-COLOUR BLOCKING

When you apply the first colour, do not fully block out the petals; instead, outline them with the first colour and leave the centres bare. Use the second colour to fill. Take care not to apply your paint too heavily.

ROTATED FLOWER WITH BLOCKED LEAVES

Using a very dry brush with a tiny amount of paint, rotate the bristles in a circular motion. This rotating action leaves enough paint on the surface for a lighter, softer look than a block application. Use the same effect in a darker colour on the inside of the petals.

ROTATING AND SHADING

Using a very dry brush with a tiny amount of paint, place your brush on one side of the stencil and rotate the brush in circles. Repeat, using a slightly darker colour on the edges, for soft shading.

ROTATING AND SHADING IN TWO COLOURS

This is similar to rotating and shading, but is more directional. Using a very dry brush with a tiny amount of paint, place your brush in the centre of the flower and rotate the bristles slightly outwards. Repeat, using a slightly darker colour.

9 5

ROTATING BRUSH WITH LEAVES FLICKED

Fill in the petals by rotating a very dry brush and a tiny amount of paint. For the flicking effect on the leaves, use slightly more paint on the brush. Working from the centre, flick the paint outwards once or twice. Do not overdo.

DRY BRUSHING, ROTATING FROM EDGE

Using big circular strokes, work from the outside of the whole stencil, moving inwards. This should leave you with more paint on the outside, as there will be less and less paint on your brush as you move.

BRUSHING UP AND DOWN FROM SIDES

This is similar to flicking. Using slightly more paint on your brush than you would for rotating, brush up and down, then from side to side. Keep your lines vertical and horizontal to give a lined effect.

BRUSHING UP AND DOWN

Using slightly more paint on your brush than you would for rotating, brush up and down only, taking care to keep your lines vertical.

DRY BRUSHING WITH CURVE

Using the rotating technique, start at the centre and work outwards in big circles.

DRY BRUSHING AND ROTATING

Apply a tiny amount of paint by rotating the bristles from the centre, and from the outside tips, to give more paint in these areas. Work along the line, using less pressure than on the centre and the tips. This gives a softer effect on the areas in between.

ROUGH STIPPLING

This method uses more paint and less pressure than rotating or flicking. Taking a reasonable amount of paint on the bristles of your brush, simply place it down lightly. This gives a rougher look. Do not go over it too many times as this spoils the effect.

TWO-COLOUR STIPPLING

Use less paint than for rough stippling. The second colour is stippled out from the centre, to blend.

ONE-SIDED STIPPLING

Apply the lighter colour first, up to a point just past the centre. Apply the darker colour, and stipple to the centre. Always start on the outer edge so that you leave more paint on the edges of the stencil design.

DRY BRUSH STIPPLING

This is similar to stippling, except that it is essential to dab most of the paint off the bristles before you start. This gives a softer stippling effect.

GENTLE STIPPLING FROM EDGE

Using a very dry brush (dab most of the paint off the bristles before you start), stipple from the outside, working inwards. By the time you get to the centre, there should be hardly any paint left on your brush, ensuring a very soft paint effect in this area.

STIPPLING TO SHADE WITH TWO COLOURS

Using a reasonable amount of paint, apply the lighter shade first. Apply the darker shade to one side only of each window. (Here, the second colour is applied to the right-hand side). A few dabs of the darker colour paint is quite sufficient.

FLICKING UPWARD WITH BRUSH

Using a reasonable amount of paint (not too wet or too dry) on your brush, flick upwards only. This creates a line at the top of the petals and leaves.

FLICKING IN TWO DIRECTIONS

Using a reasonable amount of paint on your brush, flick up and down. Do not use too much paint as it will collect on the edges.

FLICKING FROM THE OUTSIDE TO THE CENTRE

Using a reasonable amount of paint on your brush, flick from the outside edges in to the centre of the design. Flick from the top to the centre, from the bottom to the centre, from the left to the centre, and from the right to the centre.

FLICKING FROM THE TOP TO THE CENTRE

Using a reasonable amount of paint, flick from the top edge of the window to the centre of the design, then from the bottom edge to the centre.

RIGHT-HAND DROP SHADOW

Apply the first colour, which should be your lighter shade, using a block effect. Concentrate on one side of each window (here, the right-hand side). Move the stencil slightly to the left – a few millimetres is sufficient – taking care to not move it up or down. Block again, using a darker colour.

FROSTED VASES

Give coloured or clear glass vases the designer touch using glass etching cream and reverse stencilling. The shapes are cut from sticky-backed plastic and removed after stencilling to reveal the clear outlines. Choose flowers and leaves, stripes or spots - the choice is yours. The same technique could be used to transform windows.

YOU WILL NEED
glass vase
sticky-backed plastic
scissors
rubber gloves
glass etching cream
soft paintbrush

1 Wash the vase with hot soapy water to remove any grease. Leave the vase to dry. Trace the flower and leaf templates at the back of the book and transfer them on to the back of a piece of sticky-backed plastic. Cut out the shapes with scissors.

2 Decide where you want to position the shapes on the vase, remove the backing paper and stick in place, smoothing them down.

3 Wearing rubber gloves, paint the etching cream evenly over the outside of the vase with a paintbrush, and leave to dry in a warm, dust-free area for about 30 minutes.

4 Still wearing the rubber gloves, wash the cream off the vase with warm water and leave to dry. If there are blotchy areas where the cream hasn't worked, simply paint the vase again and leave it for another 30 minutes. When you are happy with the results, peel off the sticky shapes and wash the vase again to remove any sticky smears from the plastic.

▶

5 For a smaller vase, try using just one motif. Paint on the etching cream in the same way as for the large vase and leave it for 30 minutes.

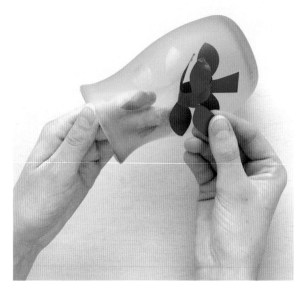

6 Wash off the etching cream and peel off the plastic motif to reveal the design, then wash the vase again.

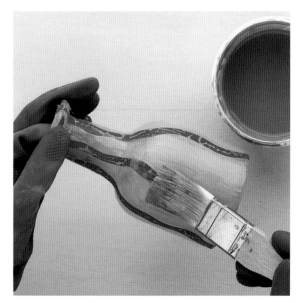

7 For a striped frosted vase, cut out straight or wiggly strips of sticky-backed plastic and stick them on to the vase. Paint on the etching cream as before and leave to dry for 30 minutes.

8 Wash off the etching cream, then peel off the plastic strips and wash the vase again to remove any sticky smears from the plastic.

ART NOUVEAU HATBOX

An elegantly stencilled hatbox and matching shoe bag would be perfect for storing a bride's hat and shoes. Make a set for yourself or to give to someone special. And you needn't stop there: stencil a whole stack of matching hatboxes to use for stylish storage in a bedroom.

YOU WILL NEED
round hatbox
white undercoat
paintbrushes
water-based woodwash in
pale green
tape measure
pencil
stencil card
craft knife and cutting mat
ruler
spray adhesive
stencil brushes
stencil paints in dark green,
royal blue and pale green

1 Paint the hatbox with two coats of white under-coat. Dilute one part pale green woodwash with one part water and apply two or three light washes to the hatbox, allowing them to dry between coats. Measure the circumference of the box and divide by six or eight. Lightly mark the measurements on the lid and side of the box with a pencil.

2 Trace the flower and heart templates at the back of the book. Cut the stencils from stencil card as described in Stencilling Techniques. Rule a pencil line across the bottom of the stencil to help align it on the box. Spray lightly with adhesive and position on the box. Using a stencil brush and dark green stencil paint, stencil the leaves and stem. Remove the stencil when dry, respray with adhesive and reposition. Continue to work around the box.

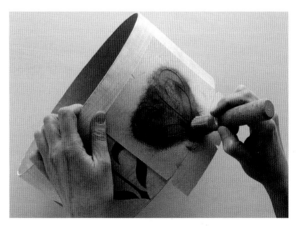

3 Reposition the stencil on the leaves, and add shadow to the points where the leaves join the stem using royal blue paint. Use a clean brush to keep the colours clean. ▶

103

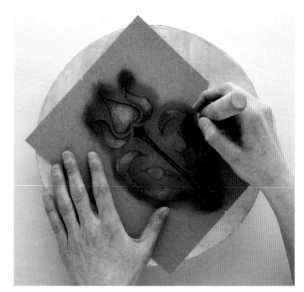

4 Using the single heart stencil, add a pale green heart between each pair of leaves.

5 Stencil flowerheads around the rim of the lid in dark green, adding a royal blue shadow as before. Stencil the flower motif in the centre of the lid.

6 Add pale green heart motifs around the main motif, using a very small amount of paint for a delicate touch.

Above: Stencil a matching calico shoe bag, using fabric paints, to protect a treasured pair of shoes.

STAR FRAME

Give plain or old picture frames a new look with textured stars. Adding ready-mixed filler to acrylic stencil paint gives a three-dimensional effect to stencilled designs. Once you have mixed your plaster you will need to work quickly before it sets.

YOU WILL NEED
wooden picture frame
emulsion paints in dark and light blue
paintbrush
soft cloth
wax furniture polish
sandpaper
acetate
craft knife and cutting mat
bowl
ready-mixed filler
acrylic paint in dark blue
stencil brush
flowerpots

1 Paint the frame in dark blue emulsion paint using a paintbrush. When dry, apply a second coat and leave to dry.

2 Using a soft cloth, rub wax furniture polish all over the frame and leave to dry.

3 Paint the frame with light blue emulsion paint and leave to dry. Paint on a second coat and leave to dry. Then lightly sand the frame to create a distressed effect.

▶

4 Cut a large and a small star stencil from acetate as described in Stencilling Techniques. In a bowl, mix together the ready-mixed filler and acrylic paint until you are happy with the shade, remembering that when the filler dries it will be much lighter.

5 Position the star stencil on the frame and dab on the filler with a stencil brush. Keep stencilling until you have covered the frame. Leave the filler to harden and wash the brush thoroughly.

6 When the filler has dried and hardened, gently smooth the stars with sandpaper.

7 Paint and stencil the flowerpots in the same way as the picture frame.

TABVLA. IN LVCEM EDITA.

MAKING SANDCASTLES

Evocative of childhood summers spent on the beach, sandcastles are simple, colourful shapes to stencil. Perfect for a child's room or for a family bathroom, they will bring a touch of humour to your walls. Paint the flags in different colours or glue on paper flags for added interest.

YOU WILL NEED
emulsion paints in blue and white
paintbrush
household sponge
acetate
craft knife and cutting mat
tape measure
pencil
masking tape
stencil paints in yellow, black and other colours of your choice
stencil brushes
fine paintbrush
coloured paper (optional)
PVA glue (optional)

1 Paint below dado-rail height in blue. When dry, rub on white emulsion with a sponge. Trace the templates at the back of the book. Cut the stencils from acetate as described in Stencilling Techniques.

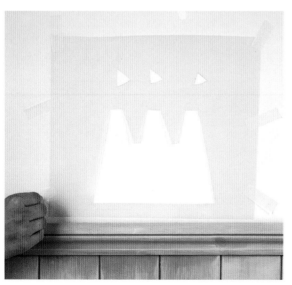

2 Measure the wall to calculate how many sand-castles you can fit on and make light pencil marks at regular intervals. Hold the stencil above the dado rail and secure the corners with masking tape.

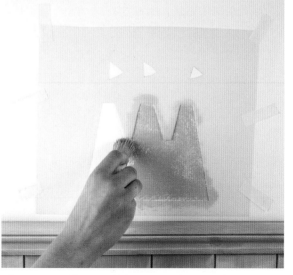

3 Using yellow stencil paint and a stencil brush, stencil in the first sandcastle.

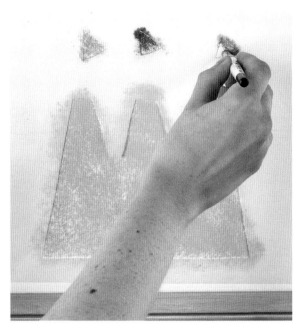

4 Stencil each flag in a different colour and remove the stencil.

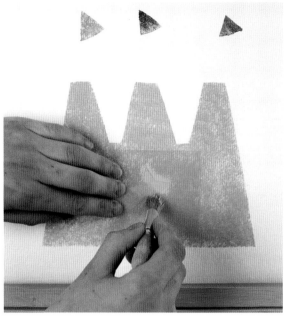

5 When the paint has dried, stencil a star on the sandcastle in a contrasting colour of paint.

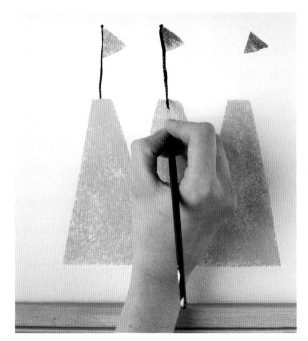

6 Using a fine paintbrush and black stencil paint, paint in the flagpoles.

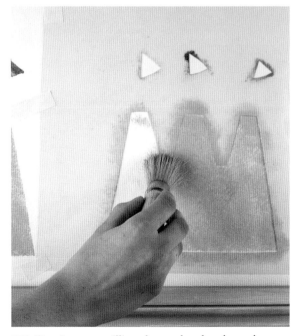

7 Continue stencilling the sandcastles along the wall using your pencil marks to position them.

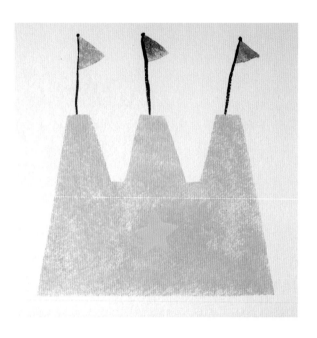

8 As an alternative to stencilling the flags, cut out
triangles of coloured paper and glue them to the
wall with PVA glue, then paint in the flagpoles.

*Above: Don't be too exacting when
painting the flagpoles. Wobbly lines
and erratic angles add to the childlike
quality of the sandcastle frieze.*

*Left: A variation on the seashore
theme might include bright tropical
shapes in Caribbean colours.*

SEASHORE BATHROOM SET

Seaside themes are always popular for a bathroom and these stencils in fresh blue and white link the different elements of the room. For best results, choose paints to suit the surface you are planning to stencil: enamel paint for plastic and glass and fabric paint for the towels.

YOU WILL NEED
acetate
craft knife and cutting mat
clear plastic shower curtain
stencil brush
enamel paints in white and blue
smooth cotton hand towel
fabric paint in dark blue
iron
2 glass tumblers
masking tape (optional)

1 Trace the shell, starfish and fish templates at the back of the book. Cut the stencils from acetate as described in the basic techniques. Lay the shower curtain on a flat surface. Lightly dab the stencil brush in the white enamel paint and begin to stencil the shapes on the curtain.

2 Continue to stencil the shapes randomly over the whole shower curtain, taking care not to overload the brush with paint. Leave to dry.

3 Reposition the stencils on the painted shapes and dab on the blue paint. Leave some of the shapes white. Leave the curtain to dry before hanging in place.

4 Lay the hand towel on a flat surface. Using the fish stencil and dark blue fabric paint, stencil a border of fish across one short edge of the towel.

5 Stencil the opposite edge of the towel, arranging the fish in a different way. Iron the towel to fix the fabric paint, following the manufacturer's instructions. ▶

6 For the glass, hold or tape the fish stencil in place and gently dab on white enamel paint.

7 Leave to dry, then reposition the stencil and continue to stencil fish all over the glass. Decorate the second glass with blue fish. The glasses should only be used for decoration; do not apply enamel paints to surfaces that will be eaten from.

Above: Blue and white stencils work well in a plain white bathroom. You can also choose colours to coordinate with your existing decor.

114

GREEK URNS

Classic Greek urns softly outlined under a warm terracotta colourwash have a very Mediterranean feel. The stencilling is worked in clear varnish so that the top colour slides over without adhering, leaving subtly coloured motifs. Arrange the urns randomly over the wall for an informal finish.

YOU WILL NEED
emulsion paints in cream and terracotta
large household sponge
acetate
craft knife and cutting mat
masking tape
stencil brush
satin acrylic varnish
wallpaper paste
cloth

1 Working in rough, sweeping strokes, rub a base coat of warm cream emulsion over the wall using a sponge. Trace the urn template at the back of the book and cut a stencil from acetate as described in the basic techniques. Tape it to the wall and stencil with clear acrylic varnish. Reposition the stencil and cover the wall with randomly arranged urns.

2 Make up the wallpaper paste following the pack instructions. Mix one part terracotta emulsion with one part paste. This will make the colourwash slimy and slow down the drying time so as to prevent "joins" in the finished colourwash. Using a sponge, dab lumps of the mixture over about 1 m/3 ft square of the wall.

3 Immediately rub the wall in a circular motion to blur the sponge marks.

▶

115

4 Continue dabbing on paint and blurring with the sponge to cover the whole wall. The varnished urns should be revealed underneath the colourwash.

5 If the urns are not clear enough, use a slightly damp cloth and your index finger to rub off a little more wash from the varnished shape. This can be done even when the wall has dried or after the room has been completed.

Left: Try colourwashing duck-egg blue over a beige background as an alternative colour combination.

PENNSYLVANIA-DUTCH TULIPS

This American folk-art inspired idea uses the rich colours and simple motifs beloved by the German and Dutch immigrants to Pennsylvania. Create the effect of hand-painted wallpaper or, for a beginner's project, take a single motif and use to decorate a key cupboard.

YOU WILL NEED
emulsion paint in dark ochre
large and small paintbrushes
woodwash in indigo blue and mulberry
stencil card
craft knife and cutting mat
pencil
ruler
stencil brushes
stencil paints in red, light green, dark green and pale brown
saucer or cloth
artist's paintbrush

1 Dilute one part ochre emulsion with one part water. Using a large paintbrush, cover the top half of the wall with the diluted emulsion. Use vertical brush strokes for an even texture.

2 Paint the lower half of the wall with indigo blue woodwash. Finish off with a curving line using a dry brush to suggest woodgrain.

3 Paint the dado rail or a strip at dado-rail height in mulberry woodwash using a narrow brush to give a clean edge.

4 Trace the tulip and heart templates at the back of the book and cut the stencils from stencil card as described in Stencilling Techniques. Mark the centre of each edge of the stencil. Measure the wall and divide it into equal sections, so that the repeats will fall at about 20 cm/8 in intervals. Mark the positions with pencil, so that they can be rubbed out later.

5 Dip the stencil brush into red stencil paint. Rub the brush on a saucer or cloth until it is almost dry before stencilling in the tulips. Leave to dry.

6 Paint the leaves in light green stencil paint with darker green shading. Paint the stems in dark green using an artist's paintbrush. Leave to dry.

7 Stencil the basket in pale brown stencil paint using a chunky stencil brush.

119

8 Stencil a single heart between each two baskets of tulips using red stencil paint.

Below: Make a matching key cupboard following the same method and using just one motif.

Above: A stencilled motif on a functional kitchen storage tin gives instant folk-art style.

FRENCH COUNTRY KITCHEN

This curtain design is adapted from the pattern on a French Art Deco soup bowl found in a fleamarket in Brussels. The flower design is also echoed in the hand-stencilled tiles and teams perfectly with the simple chequerboard border for a country look.

YOU WILL NEED

FOR THE CURTAIN:
white muslin (see measuring up)
iron
newspaper
masking tape
stencil card
craft knife and cutting mat
spray adhesive
solid stencil paint in blue
stencil brush
pressing cloth
needle
white sewing cotton
tape measure
dressmaker's chalk
white cotton tape
small pearl buttons
FOR THE TILES:
10 cm/4 in square white tiles
spray paint in red

MEASURING UP

To calculate the amount of muslin, allow 1.5 x the width of the window plus 2.5 cm/1 in for each side hem, and add 7.5 cm/3 in to the length for hems.

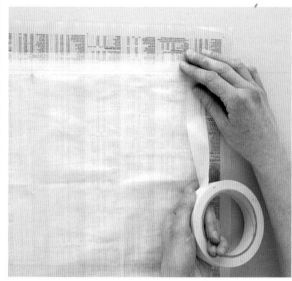

1 Press the muslin to remove any creases, then fold it lengthways in concertina folds. Press lightly to mark the creases, then fold it widthways in concertina folds and press again. These squares will act as a guide for positioning the motifs. Cover the work surface with newspaper and tape down the muslin so that it is taut.

2 Trace the three floral templates and the border template at the back of the book and cut out the stencils from stencil card as described in Stencilling Techniques. Spray the back of one stencil with adhesive and, starting at the top right, lightly stencil the first motif.

3 Alternating the stencils as you work, stencil flowers in every other square over the whole curtain, leaving 15 cm/6 in free at the lower edge.

4 Stencil the blue chequerboard border along the bottom, lining up the stencil each time by matching the last two squares of the previous motif with the first two of the next stencil. Press the fabric well using a pressing cloth and iron.

5 Press under and slip-stitch a 1.25 cm/½ in double hem around the sides and lower edge. Make a 2.5 cm/1 in double hem along the top edge.

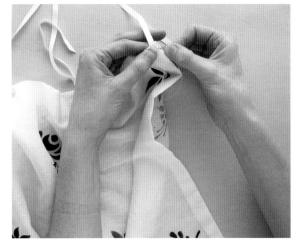

6 Measure the top edge of the curtain and, using dressmakers' chalk, mark it into sections about 20 cm/8 in apart. Cut a 25 cm/10 in piece of cotton tape for each mark. Fold the first piece of tape in half and stitch to the back of the first mark. Sew a button on to the front of the curtain to anchor the tape. Repeat all the way along the edge and then tie the finished curtain on to the curtain pole in bows. ▶

7 For the tiles, cut a piece of stencil card to fit the tile. Cut out the three floral stencils as before, using a craft knife and a cutting mat.

Above: The simple tape ties that attach the curtain to the pole make an attractively rustic finish.

8 Cover the work-surface with newspaper. Using red spray paint, spray over the stencil lightly and evenly. Leave to dry, then remove the stencil.

Above: The coordinating tiles can be used individually as pot stands or set in the wall among plain white tiles.

TRAY OF AUTUMN LEAVES

The rich colours of autumn leaves are captured here on a simple wooden tray. Keep to warm natural paint colours to suit the country style and simple lines of the tray. Use the templates provided here or draw around your own pressed leaves.

YOU WILL NEED
wooden tray
fine-grade sandpaper
water-based primer (if bare wood)
emulsion paints in blue-grey and ochre
paintbrushes
household candle
cloth
stencil card
craft knife and cutting mat
spray adhesive
stencil brush
stencil paints in rust and terracotta
saucer
matt acrylic varnish

1 Sand down the tray with fine-grade sandpaper to ensure a smooth surface. If the wood is bare, paint with a water-based primer. Apply two coats of blue-grey paint, leaving it to dry between coats.

2 Rub the candle over the edges of the tray and over the base until there is a build-up of wax. Think about which areas of the tray would become worn naturally and apply wax there.

3 Wipe away any loose bits of wax. Paint the whole tray with the ochre paint and leave to dry completely.

127

4 Lightly rub over the tray with sandpaper to reveal some of the blue-grey paint underneath.

5 Trace the templates at the back of the book or draw around pressed leaves. Cut out the stencils from card as described in Stencilling Techniques.

Above: Building up layers of paint and rubbing back the top layer in places gives the tray a pleasing distressed look.

6 Lightly spray the back of the stencils with adhesive. Arrange the stencils on the tray and smooth down. Dip the stencil brush into the rust stencil paint and rub it on a saucer or cloth so that the brush is dry. Using circular movements, apply the colour evenly over the stencils, working more on one side of each motif. Apply terracotta paint to the other side of the leaves to give shadow. Continue stencilling all over the tray. To give the tray a tough finish, apply two or three coats of varnish, leaving each coat to dry before applying the next.

GILDED CANDLES

Plain church candles look extra special when adorned with simple gold stars and stripes. Always associated with Christmas, candles are popular all year round for their soft romantic lighting. Cutting the stencils may be fiddly but it is then a quick job to spray on the gold paint.

YOU WILL NEED
acetate
selection of candles
marker pen
craft knife and cutting mat
spray adhesive
masking tape
metallic spray paint

1 Wrap a piece of acetate around the candle. Mark and cut it to fit exactly. Do not overlap the edges. Cut it a few millimetres shorter than the candle.

2 Trace the star templates at the back of the book. Lay a piece of acetate over the stars and trace over them with a marker pen.

3 Cut out the stars using a craft knife and cutting mat. Be careful not to tear the acetate.

4 Spray one side of the stencil with adhesive and wrap around the candle, centring it so that there is a small gap at either end. Secure the acetate join with masking tape. Mask the top of the candle with tape, ensuring there are no gaps. ▶

129

5 Spray a fine mist of metallic spray paint over the candle, holding the can about 30 cm/ 12 in from the surface. If too much paint is applied, it will drip underneath the stencil. Keep checking that the stencil is well stuck down to avoid any fuzzy lines around the stars. Leave the paint to dry for a couple of minutes, then carefully remove the masking tape and acetate.

6 For a stars and stripes candle, cut strips of acetate and trace a line of small stars along each strip. Cut out with a craft knife as before. Spray one side of the acetate strips with adhesive. Stick the strips on to the candle, measuring the gaps in between to ensure equal spacing. Secure them with small pieces of masking tape at the join.

7 Mask off the top of the candle as before. Spray the candle with metallic paint and remove the masking tape and stencil when dry.

8 For a reverse stencil design, cut out individual star shapes from acetate. Apply spray adhesive to one side, stick on to the candle and mask off the top of the candle as before. Spray with metallic paint and carefully remove the acetate stars when the paint is dry.

Above: A basketful of starry gilded candles makes a pretty gift.

RENAISSANCE ART

Turn your hallway into a dramatic entrance with ornate stencils and rich colours. Combine them with gold accessories, velvets and braids to complete the theatrical setting. This design would also be ideal for creating an intimate dining room for candlelit dinners.

YOU WILL NEED
ruler
spirit level
pencil
masking tape
emulsion paints in pale slate-blue, terracotta
and pale peach
sponges
stencil brushes
stencil card
craft knife and cutting mat
stencil paints in dark grey-blue, terracotta,
emerald and turquoise

1 Using a ruler and spirit level, divide the wall in half horizontally with a pencil line, then draw a second line 15 cm/6 in above the first. Stick a line of masking tape just below this top line. Dilute one part slate-blue emulsion with one part water and colour the top half of the wall using a sponge.

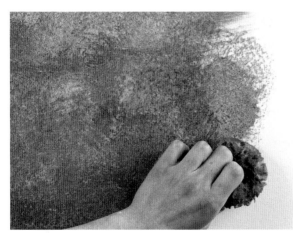

2 Stick masking tape just above the bottom pencil line. Dilute terracotta emulsion with water and sponge over the lower half of the wall.

3 Sponge lightly over the terracotta with slate-blue to add a textural effect. Remove the strips of masking tape.

4 Colour the centre band with diluted peach emulsion using a stencil brush. Trace the templates at the back of the book and cut out the stencils from stencil card.

5 Stencil the wall motifs at roughly regular intervals over the upper part of the wall, using dark grey-blue. Rotate the stencil with every alternate motif to give movement to the design.

6 Starting at the right-hand side of the peach band, stencil the border motif with terracotta stencil paint. Add details in emerald and turquoise. Continue along the wall, positioning the stencil beside the previous motif so that the spaces are equal.

Right: Make a matching patchwork cushion cover with pieces of fabric stencilled with gold fabric paint. Add offcuts of velvet and cover all the seams with ornate trimmings.

GEOMETRIC FLOOR TILES

This repeating pattern is derived from an ancient Greek mosaic floor. Cork floor tiles take colour well - only use a small amount of paint and build it up in layers if necessary. Make two stencils, one for each colour, so that the colours do not get mixed.

YOU WILL NEED
graph paper
ruler
pencil
compass
stencil card
craft knife and cutting mat
masking tape
30 cm /12 in cork tiles
spray adhesive
stencil paints in terracotta and blue
stencil brushes
acrylic sealer

1 Enlarge the quarter section template at the back of the book so that it will fit within a 15 cm/ 6 in square. Using graph paper will make the design more accurate. Rule the three squares and draw the curves with a compass. Rub over all the pencil lines on the back with a pencil.

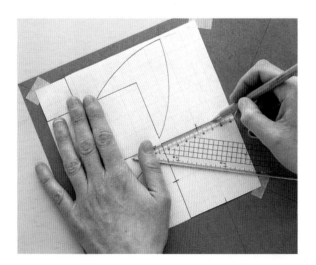

2 Cut two 30 cm/12 in squares from stencil card and draw four lines, from corner to corner and edge to edge, to divide each card into eight equal segments. For the first stencil, tape the paper face up to one corner of the first card and draw around the corner and centre square to transfer the design to the card. Repeat on each corner, turning the paper 90° each time. Cut out the five squares. For the second stencil, draw along the curves and around the remaining square. Cut out these eight shapes.

3 Wipe the tile to remove any cork dust and coat the back of the first stencil with spray adhesive. Stencil the squares using terracotta stencil paint and a stencil brush.

4 Leave to dry, then use the second stencil and blue paint to complete the design. Stencil the remaining tiles in the same way.

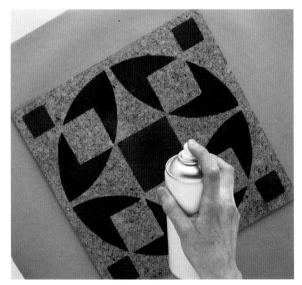

5 When all the tiles are complete, spray with acrylic sealer to make them waterproof. Fix them to the floor following the manufacturer's instructions.

Above: Make half the tiles in different colours to make a chequerboard-patterned floor.

Right: A gentle shading of blue has been added to the yellow shapes and yellow to the blue shapes to give a softer outline to the design.

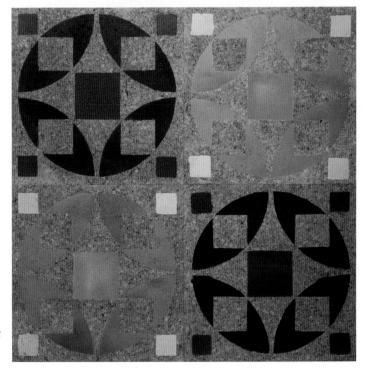

Right: Different colour combinations create quite different effects. When using more than two colours, you will either need to cut more stencils or to mask out the area that will be coloured differently.

ORGANZA CUSHION

If you always thought stencilling had a simple country look, then think again. This brilliant organza cushion with gold stencilling takes the craft into the luxury class. Use the sharpest dressmaker's pins when handling organza to avoid marking the fabric.

YOU WILL NEED
dressmaker's graph paper
ruler
pencil
scissors
dressmaker's pins
organza, 1 m/1⅛ yd each in main
colour and contrast colour
stencil card
craft knife and cutting mat
spray adhesive
scrap paper
masking tape
gold spray paint
needle and thread
sewing machine
iron
50 cm/20 in cushion pad

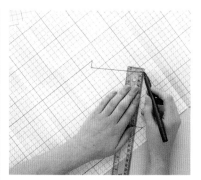

1 Copy the border template at the back of the book on to dressmaker's graph paper and cut it out. In addition, cut out a 53 cm/21 in square and a 53 x 40 cm/21 x 16 in rectangle from graph paper.

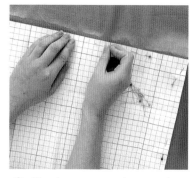

2 Pin the square and rectangle to the main colour organza. Cut two 53 cm /21 in squares, and two rectangles measuring 53 x 40 cm/21 x 16 in from the main fabric. Cut four border pieces from the contrasting fabric.

3 Cut a piece of stencil card 18 x 53 cm/7 x 21 in. Trace the template and transfer to the card, 8 cm/3 in from the bottom edge and with 6 cm/2½ in to spare at each end. Cut out the stencil.

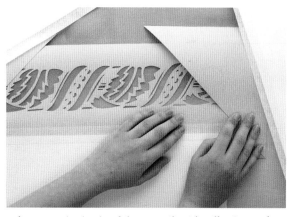

4 Spray the back of the stencil with adhesive and position along the edge of the main organza fabric square. Cut two 45° mitres from stencil card, spray with adhesive and press in place. Mask off the surrounding areas with scrap paper.

▶

141

5 Spray with gold paint. Leave to dry and spray again. Remove the masking paper and stencil. Place the stencil along the next edge, put the mitres in place and continue as before. Stencil the remaining two sides. Hem one long edge of each fabric rectangle by folding over 1 cm/⅜ in, then 1.5 cm/⅝ in. Pin, tack and machine stitch the hem, then press.

6 Lay the stencilled fabric square face down and the second square on top. Lay the two rectangles on top of these, overlapping the stitched edges so that the raw edges line up with the square pieces. Pin, tack and machine stitch 1 cm/⅜ in from the raw edge. Trim seam allowance to 7 mm/¼ in. Pin, tack and stitch the border pieces together at the mitred corners 1.3 cm/½ in from the raw edges. Trim the corners and turn the right way out. Press. Continue until the border pieces make a ring.

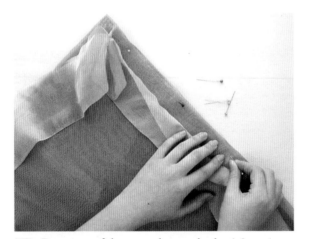

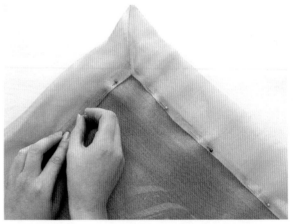

7 Press one of the raw edges under by 1.3 cm/½ in. Lay the pressed edge of the border fabric along the edge of the main fabric square and pin, tack and stitch in place.

8 Turn the cushion over and pull the border over. Turn under the border's raw edge by 1.3 cm/½ in and pin in place along the front of the cushion. Tack and stitch in place. Press. Insert the cushion pad.

TABLECLOTH AND NAPKINS

Inspiration for stencil designs can be all around you, waiting to be discovered. Cutlery and kitchen utensils are wonderful graphic shapes, ideal for stencilling. Arrange them as borders around the edge of a cloth or place them formally on each side of an imaginary place setting.

YOU WILL NEED
acetate
craft knife and cutting mat
plain-coloured cotton napkins
and tablecloth
fabric paints in various colours
stencil brush
fine artist's paintbrush
iron

1 Trace the cutlery, heart and utensils templates at the back of the book and cut the stencils from acetate. Lay one of the napkins on a flat surface. Plan your design and start to stencil around the edge of the napkin.

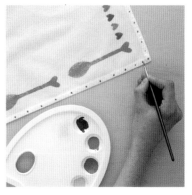

2 Stencil hearts in between the cutlery stencils. Using a fine artist's paintbrush, paint dots around the hem of the napkins.

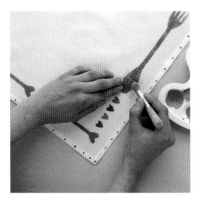

3 With the stencil brush stencil hearts on the handles of some of the cutlery.

4 Stencil each napkin with a different pattern, varying the arrangement of the stencils.

5 Lay the tablecloth on a flat surface and begin to stencil the border of cutlery and hearts.

▶

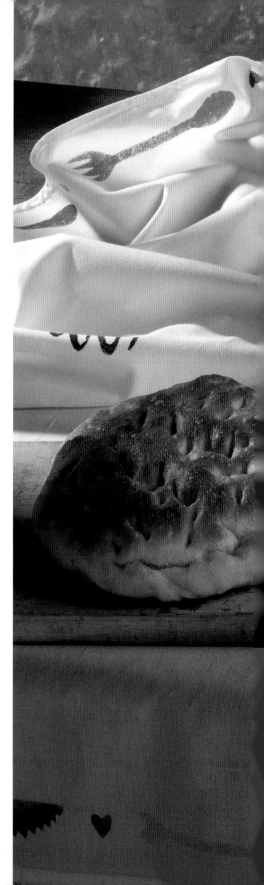

6 Stencil the larger utensil shapes in the middle of the tablecloth. Stencil the handles first. Paint the top of the utensils, for example the whisk, in a contrasting colour.

7 Stencil the draining spoons and then add the draining holes in a different colour.

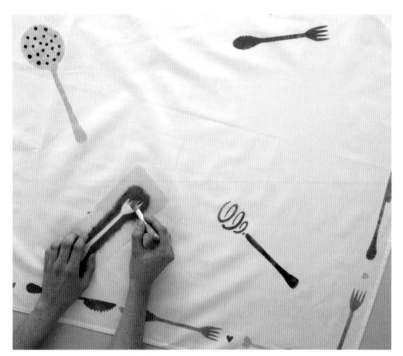

8 Fill in the areas around the utensils with more cutlery stencils. Leave the fabric paint to dry and then iron the reverse of the fabric to fix the paint.

THROUGH THE GRAPEVINE

This classic grape stencil will bring back holiday memories of sipping Greek wine under a canopy of vines. The stencilled grapes are all the more effective set against the purple and green dry-brushed walls. Practise your paint effects on small boards before tackling full-scale walls.

YOU WILL NEED
large paintbrush
emulsion paints in purple and green
pencil
ruler
spirit level
acetate
craft knife and cutting mat
masking tape
stencil paint in purple and lilac
stencil brush
silver gilt cream
soft cloth

1 Dip the end of a large paintbrush in purple emulsion, scrape off the excess and apply to the wall, brushing in varying directions and not completely covering the wall. This process is known as dry-brushing.

2 Repeat the process with green emulsion, filling in some of the gaps.

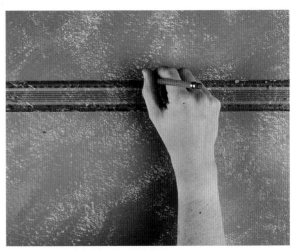

3 Draw a horizontal pencil line at the desired height on the wall using a ruler and spirit level.

4 Trace the grape stencil at the back of the book and cut the stencil from acetate. Tape the stencil in place with its top edge on the pencil line. Apply purple stencil paint over the whole stencil.

5 Add lilac stencil paint at the bottom of each window in the stencil to create highlights.

6 Dip the stencil brush in the silver gilt cream, brush off any excess and brush over the design using an up and down movement.

7 Select a few leaf shapes from the stencil and mask off. Position randomly over the wall and stencil in purple. Brush over with the gilt cream. (They are too small to require the lilac highlight.)

▶

8 Leave the stencilling to dry overnight. With a soft cloth, buff up the silver cream to a shine.

ROPE AND SHELLS

The chunky rope cleverly linking the seashells is echoed by individual stencilled knots. Shells are always popular motifs for a bathroom design and look good in many colour combinations, from nautical blue and white to greens and aquas or pinks and corals.

YOU WILL NEED
large household sponges
emulsion paints in nautical blue and white
ruler
spirit level
pencil
acetate
craft knife and cutting mat
masking tape
stencil paints in dark blue, light blue and camel
stencil brush
rubber
cloth

1 Using a household sponge rub nautical blue emulsion paint over the wall to create a very rough and patchy finish. Leave to dry.

2 Using a clean sponge, rub a generous amount of white emulsion over the wall so that it almost covers the blue, giving a slightly mottled effect.

3 Using a ruler and spirit level, draw a horizontal pencil line at the desired height of the border. Trace the seashore and knot templates at the back of the book and cut the stencils from acetate. Position the seashore stencil with its top edge on the pencil line and secure with masking tape. Stencil dark blue paint around the edges of the shells and seaweed, using a stencil brush.

4 Using light blue stencil paint, shade in the shells, the seaweed and the recesses of the rope.

5 Using the camel stencil paint, fill in the remainder of the rope and highlight the shells and seaweed. Continue to stencil the shell and rope border right around the room.

6 Draw a vertical line from each loop of rope to the skirting board. Starting 30 cm/12 in from the border, make pencil marks at 30cm/12 in intervals down the line to mark the positions of the knots. Start every alternate line of marks 15 cm/6 in below the border so that the knots will be staggered. ▶

151

7 Tape the knotted rope stencil on to the first pencil mark. Stencil dark blue in the recesses of the rope.

8 Stencil the remainder of the rope in camel. Leave to dry. Remove any visible pencil marks with a rubber and wipe over with a slightly damp cloth.

Left: Create a variation on the sea theme by stencilling a row of starfish at dado-rail height.

HERALDIC DINING ROOM

Lend an atmosphere of medieval luxury to your dining room with richly coloured walls and heraldic motifs stencilled in the same deep tones. Gilt accessories, heavy fabrics and a profusion of candles team well with this decor. All that remains is to prepare a sumptuous banquet.

YOU WILL NEED
large household sponges
emulsion paints in camel, deep red and deep purple
ruler
spirit level
pencil
masking tape
acetate
craft knife and cutting mat
stencil brush
fine lining brush

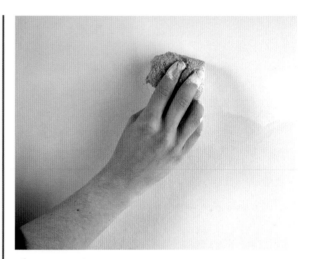

1 Using a large household sponge, rub camel emulsion all over the wall. Leave to dry.

2 Repeat the process using a generous amount of deep red emulsion so that it almost covers the camel, giving a slightly mottled effect. Leave to dry.

3 Using a ruler and spirit level, draw a pencil line at dado-rail height and stick a line of masking tape just above it.

4 Sponge deep purple emulsion all over the wall below the masking tape to give a slightly mottled effect. Leave to dry, then remove the masking tape.

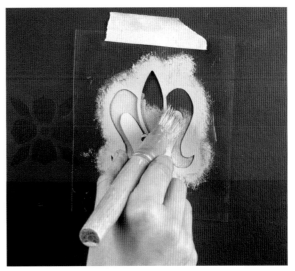

5 Trace the heraldic templates at the back of the book and cut the stencils from acetate. Secure the rose stencil above the dividing line and stencil in purple emulsion, using the stencil brush. When dry, position the fleur-de-lys stencil next to the rose and stencil in camel emulsion. Continue to alternate the stencils around the room.

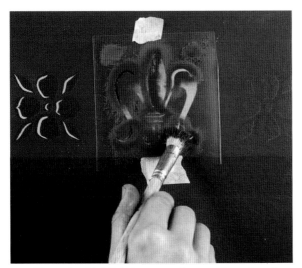

6 Place the highlighting stencils over the painted motifs and, with a stencil brush, add purple highlights to the camel fleurs-de-lys and camel highlights to the purple roses.

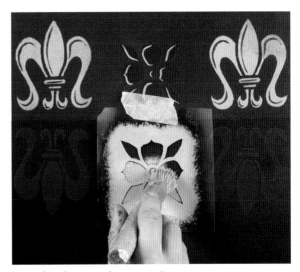

7 Flip the stencils over and position as mirror images below the previously stencilled motifs. Stencil the roses in camel and the fleurs-de-lys in red.

155

8 Add highlights as before, using camel on the fleurs-de-lys and purple on the camel roses.

9 Using a fine lining brush and camel paint, paint a narrow line where the red and purple paints meet. If you do not have the confidence to do this freehand, position two rows of masking tape on the wall, leaving a small gap in between. When the line of paint is dry, carefully remove the masking tape.

TROMPE-L'ŒIL PLATES

A shelf full of decorative painted plates adds a witty touch to a kitchen corner. Follow these plate designs or translate your own patterned china into stencils to give a co-ordinated look. Why not add some individual plates to the wall as well?

YOU WILL NEED
stencil card
pencil
ruler
craft knife and cutting mat
23 cm/9 in diameter plate
compass
spray adhesive
newspaper or brown paper
masking tape
spray paints in white, cream, a
range of pinks and mauves, light
green, dark green, red, blue and grey

1 Cut three pieces of stencil card 30 cm/12 in square. Mark the centre of each card by measuring the centre of each edge and ruling a horizontal and a vertical line across each card to join the marks.

2 Draw a line 3.5 cm/1¼ in in from all four edges of each card. Place the plate in the centre of the card and draw around the edge. Cut out the plate shape from the first piece of stencil card (stencil 1).

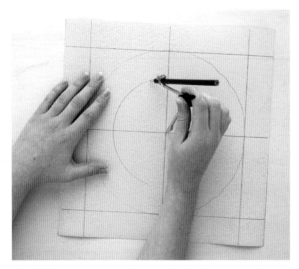

3 Using a compass, draw a circle about 4 cm/ 1½ in from the edge of the plate on the two remaining pieces of card.

4 Trace or photocopy the plate template at the back of the book to the desired size and transfer to the second stencil card.

5 Cut out the design with a craft knife on a cutting mat. Cut out the smaller areas first and the larger areas last (stencil 2). On the third piece of stencil card, cut out the inner circle (stencil 3).

6 Draw a faint horizontal pencil line on the wall and put two marks 30 cm/12 in apart on the line to act as a guide for positioning the stencils. Spray the back of the plate stencil (1) with adhesive and place in position on the wall. Press down firmly to ensure a good contact. Mask off the surrounding area with paper and masking tape, leaving no gaps. Spray white and cream spray paint on to the stencil. Remove the masks and stencil.

7 Attach the flower stencil (2) to the wall with spray adhesive, lining it up with the marks on the wall. Mask off the surrounding area. Stick small pieces of masking tape over the leaves on the stencil. Spray the flowers with pinks and mauves, applying a fine layer of paint in short sharp puffs. Try each paint colour on the mask surrounding the stencil to test the colour and to make sure that the nozzle is clear.

8 Remove the masking tape from the leaves. Fold a small piece of card in half and use it to shield the rest of the stencil from paint. Spray the leaves using light and dark green paints, trying not to get too much green on the flowers.

9 Cut a small hole in a piece of card and use to spray the centres of the flowers green.

10 Hold the shield of card around the dot designs on the border, and spray each one with red paint. Spray blue paint over the wavy lines on the border. Again, do not apply too much paint. Remove the masks and carefully remove the stencil. ▶

11 Spray the back of the last stencil (3) with adhesive and position on the wall. Mask off the surrounding area as before. Spray an extremely fine mist of grey paint over the top left-hand side and bottom right-hand side of the plate design to create a shadow. Aim the nozzle slightly away from the stencil to ensure that hardly any paint hits the wall. Remove the masks and stencil.

12 Reposition stencil 1 on the wall and spray a very fine mist of blue paint around the edge of the plate. Repeat all stages along the edge of the shelf length.

CELESTIAL CHERUBS

This exuberant baroque decoration is perfect for a sumptuous bedroom.
The cherubs are stencilled in metallic shades of bronze, gold and copper, but you could use
plain colours for a simpler result that would be suitable for a child's room.

YOU WILL NEED
emulsion paints in white, blue and grey
paintbrush
sponge
stencil card
craft knife and cutting mat
masking tape
stencil paints in gold, copper, bronze and white
stencil brush

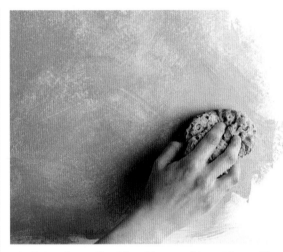

1 Paint the wall with white emulsion. Next, dilute one part blue emulsion with one part water, and, using a sponge, lightly apply it to the wall.

2 Sponge in a few areas of grey to give the impression of a cloudy sky. Sponge in a few pale areas by mixing a little white into the grey paint to suggest the edges of clouds.

3 Trace the cherub and heart templates at the back of the book and cut the stencils from stencil card. Secure the cherub stencil to the wall with masking tape. Stencil the body of the cherub in gold.

162

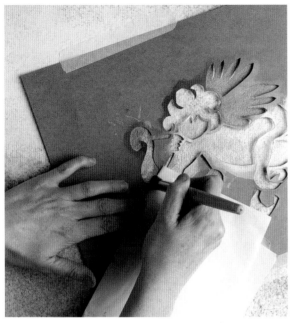

4 Stencil the wings and bow in copper, covering the adjacent parts of the stencil with scrap paper.

5 Stencil the hair and arrow in bronze.

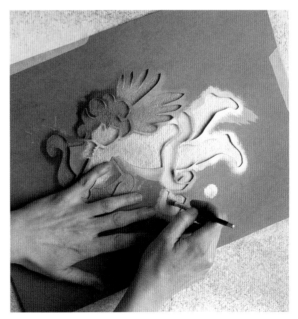

6 Stencil the drape in white with some bronze shadows.

7 To give a three-dimensional effect to the whole design, add bronze shadows at the edges of the various parts of the motif.

8 Stencil more cherubs, varying the design by reversing the card sometimes. Stencil the inter-linked hearts in the spaces using bronze paint.

Right: Try to position the stencils so that the cupids are aiming their arrows at the interlinked hearts − perfect for a romantic bedroom.

STAMPING

Although stamping is often regarded as a type of stencilling, it is basically a very easy form of printing and produces a very different finished effect. You can make your own stamps from household sponges, or buy commercial stamps in a variety of shapes and sizes. It is a quick and effective technique – all you need is the stamp, a prepared surface and your imagination.

As long as the surface is firm enough to take the pressure of the stamp, you can add details to almost anything, from walls to wrapping paper. The most successful results are achieved by holding the stamp steady and not letting it slide. This will take a little practice, so it is often helpful to use a plain sheet of paper first. Once the basic stamp has been applied, you may want to add further details with freehand painting, or simply apply more colours to the design. With enough practice, you will be able to stamp around curves to achieve particularly sophisticated effects.

STAMPING MATERIALS

Different paints and stamps will produce very different results.

DUTCH METAL LEAF AND GOLD SIZE
Metal leaf is a cheap, easy-to-use alternative to real gold leaf. Use a sponge stamp to apply gold size in a repeating pattern. When the size is tacky, apply the gold leaf.

INKS
Water-based inks are too runny to use on their own but can be added to wallpaper paste or varnish to make a mixture thick enough to adhere to the stamp. Use them for paper or card, but not for walls. If you are using rubber stamps, inkpads are commercially available in a wide range of colours.

INTERIOR FILLER (SPACKLE)
Add filler, in its dry powdered state, to emulsion paint to give it body without diluting the colour.

PAINT
Water-based paints such as emulsion (latex) and artist's acrylics dry quickly to a perma-nent finish. Use emulsion paint straight from the can or dilute it with wallpaper paste or varnish. For wall treatments, emulsion paint can be thinned with water and sponged or brushed over the wall as a colourwash.

PRECUT STAMPS
Rubber stamps are widely avail-able in thousands of designs.

Finely detailed motifs are best suited to small-scale projects, while bolder shapes are best for walls and furniture.

SPONGE OR FOAM
Different types of sponge are characterized by their density. High-density sponge is best for detailed shapes and will give a smooth, sharp print. Medium-density sponge or low-density sponge will absorb more paint and give a more textured result.

VARNISH
Use water-based, acrylic varnish (sold as quick-drying) for stamping projects. It can be mixed with emulsion paint or ink to thicken the texture and create a range of different sheens.

WALLPAPER PASTE
Wallpaper paste allows you to thin emulsion paint without making it too runny to adhere to the stamp. Mix up the paste with the required amount of water first, then add the emulsion.

Opposite: Dutch metal leaf and gold size (1); coloured inks (2); low-density sponge (3); precut stamp (4); high-density sponge (5); medium-density sponges (6); interior filler (spackle) (7); emulsion (latex) paint (8); varnish (9); wallpaper paste (10).

8

STAMPING EQUIPMENT

Stamping does not require a great deal of specialist equipment;
many of the items used are found in most households.

CRAFT KNIFE

A sharp-bladed craft knife is essential for cutting your own stamps out of sponge. Use a cutting mat to protect your work surface, and always direct the blade away from your fingers.

LINO BLOCKS

Lino blocks are available from art and craft shops and can be cut to make stamps which recreate the look of a wood block. You'll need special lino-cutting tools, which are also easily available, to scoop out the areas around the design. Always hold the lino with your spare hand behind your cutting hand for safety.

MASKING TAPE

Use for masking off areas of walls and furniture when painting.

NATURAL SPONGE

Use for applying colourwashes to walls before stamping.

PAINTBRUSHES

A range of decorator's brushes is needed for painting furniture and walls before stamping. Use a broad brush to apply colourwashes to walls. Stiff brushes can be used to stipple paint on to stamps for textured effects, while finer brushes are used to pick out details or to apply paint to the stamp.

PENCILS, PENS AND CRAYONS

Use a soft pencil to trace templates for stamps, and for making easily removable guidelines on walls. Draw motifs freehand using a marker pen on medium- and low-density sponge. Use a white crayon on black upholstery foam.

RAGS

Keep a stock of clean rags and cloths for cleaning stamps and preparing surfaces.

RULER AND TAPE MEASURE

Use these to plan your design.

SCISSORS

Use sharp scissors to cut out medium- and low-density sponge shapes and for cutting out templates.

SPONGE ROLLERS

Small paint rollers can be used to load your stamps. You will need several if you are stamping in different colours.

Opposite: scissors (1); craft knife (2); masking tape (3); paint rollers (4); ruler (5); tape measure (6); pencils (7); cutting mat (8); rag (9); natural sponge (10); paintbrushes (11).

STAMPING TECHNIQUES

Stamping is a quick and effective method of repeating a design on a wide variety of surfaces, using many different mixtures of paints and inks. Ready-made stamps are widely available, usually mounted on wooden blocks, but they are also easy to make yourself using foam or sponge.

MAKING STAMPS

1 Use high-density sponge for sharply defined and detailed designs. Trace your chosen motif on to the sponge using a soft pencil for dark, clear lines.

2 Roughly cut around the design, then spray the tracing paper with adhesive to hold it in place on the sponge while you are cutting it out.

3 Cut along the outline using a sharp blade, then, pinching the background sections, cut them away holding the blade away from your fingers.

4 The surface of low-density sponge is too soft to use tracing paper; it is easier to draw the design straight on to the sponge using a marker pen.

5 Sharp scissors can be used with this material and are especially useful for cutting out the basic shapes.

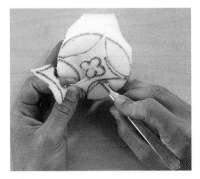

6 As with high-density sponge, the unwanted background areas should be cut away with a craft knife when the outline has been cut, but care is needed as this sponge will tear more easily. Rinse the completed stamp to remove the remains of the marker ink.

PAINT MIXTURES

WALLPAPER PASTE AND EMULSION (LATEX) PAINT

Add 50% paste to the paint to give a watercolour effect without producing a mixture that is too runny to work with. Apply using a roller, sponge or paintbrush, or dip the stamp into the paint on a flat plate.

WALLPAPER PASTE AND INK

Wallpaper paste thickens the texture of ink, while keeping the rich colour. The effect produced depends on the proportion of ink in the mixture. It will give a more even spread of colour than using emulsion. Apply using a roller or paintbrush.

VARNISH AND EMULSION PAINT

The density of the paint is diluted as with wallpaper paste, but this can also be used to create different sheens according to the type of varnish used. Apply with a roller, paintbrush or sponge, or dip the stamp into the paint on a plate.

VARNISH AND INK

This effect is similar to the wallpaper paste mixture, but creates a smoother mix as both materials are fine in texture. Again, different sheens can be obtained. Apply with a roller.

WALLPAPER PASTE AND WOODSTAIN

The paste dilutes the colour density of the stain while thickening the mixture for ease of use. Use quick-drying, water-based woodstains. Apply with a roller.

INTERIOR FILLER AND EMULSION PAINT

This mixture thickens the paint as opposed to diluting the colour, and is good for creating relief effects. Apply generously, using a paintbrush, or dip the stamp into the paint on a plate.

HOW TO APPLY PAINT

USING A ROLLER

Pour a little paint on to the side of a flat plate, then, using a sponge roller, pick up a small amount and roll it out over the rest of the plate until you have an even covering. Roll the paint on to the stamp.

USING A PAINTBRUSH

Use a fairly stiff brush and apply the paint with a dabbing or stippling motion. This technique enables more than one colour to be applied and for detail to be picked out. Be careful not to over-load the stamp, as this may cause it to slip when stamping.

DIPPING INTO PAINT ON A PLATE

Brush a thin coat of paint on to a flat plate, then press the stamp into the paint. You may need to do this several times to get an even coating. Initially the stamp will absorb a good amount of paint. Keep brushing more paint on to the plate.

USING A ROLLER AND BRUSH

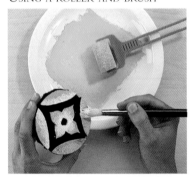

Use a sponge roller to apply the paint evenly over the whole stamp. Use a brush to apply a second colour to act as a highlight or shadow, or to pick out details of the design.

USING A SPONGE

Spread the paint on a plate, then use a natural sponge to pick up the paint and dab it on to the stamp. This method allows you to put a light, even covering of paint on to the stamp.

USING AN INKSTAMP PAD

Press the stamp on to the inkpad several times to ensure a good covering. This technique will give a dry look to the stamp.

PREPARING SURFACES

TILES, CHINA AND GLASS

These are all prepared in the same way, using soapy water to remove dirt and grease, then drying with a lint-free cloth. Appropriate specialist paints must be used as normal emulsion (latex) and acrylic paints will not adhere well and are not sufficiently durable for these surfaces.

1 Wash the tile or glass with soapy water and rinse thoroughly. To remove any remaining traces of grease, give the surface a final wipe with a cloth dipped in methylated spirits and leave·to dry.

2 When printing on a curved surface, carefully roll the stamp while holding the object securely. Sponge stamps are best suited for this purpose. Rubber stamps are less suitable.

FABRICS

Fabrics must be washed and ironed before stamping to remove any dressing and allow for any shrinkage. Again, use specialist fabric paint so that the item can be washed. Fix the paint according to the manufacturer's instructions.

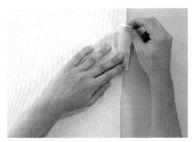

1 Once ironed, lay the fabric on a flat surface and tape the edges to hold it steady.

2 Place a piece of cardboard or scrap paper under the area to be stamped to stop any paint bleeding through the fabric.

WOOD

Wood should be lightly sanded before stamping and varnished afterwards. When using wood-stains, keep the stamp quite dry to stop the stain bleeding into the grain of the wood.

1 Sand the surface and wipe down with a soft cloth to remove any loose dust.

2 Once dry, the stamped design can be rubbed back to create a distressed effect.

175

PLANNING A DESIGN

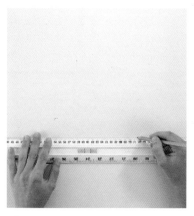

1 With the aid of a spirit level (carpenter's level), draw a faint pencil line to use as a guide when stamping.

2 Stamp the motif several times on scrap paper and cut out the prints. Tape them to the wall so that you can judge how your design will look.

3 When using a stamp mounted on a block, you can draw a straight line on the back to help with positioning. Align the block with the pencil guideline on the wall.

4 A piece of cardboard held between the previous print and the stamp will ensure consistent spacing between motifs.

5 For a tighter look, butt the stamped motifs together.

6 Once the paint is dry, the pencil guideline can be removed using a cloth wrung out in soapy water and rubbed along the line.

STAMP EFFECTS

You can achieve many different effects with stamps, depending on the paint mixture you use and the way it is applied. The same stamp, cut from high-density sponge, was used to make all these prints.

HALF-SHADE

Roll the first, paler colour over the stamp, then roll a second, darker shade over one half only, to create a three-dimensional shadowed effect.

TWO-TONE

Using a dry roller, load the stamp with the first colour, then apply the second to the top and bottom edges only.

TWO-TONE WITH DRY ROLLER

For an even subtler colour mix, roll the second colour right over the first using a very dry roller.

CONTRASTING DETAIL

Pick out details of the design in a contrasting colour: apply the first colour with a roller, then use a brush to apply the second colour in the areas you want.

PARTIAL OUTLINE

This shadow effect is produced by stamping the motif in one colour, then partially outlining the print using a paintbrush or felt-tip pen.

DROP SHADOW

Another, very subtle, effect of shadows and highlights is produced by printing the motif in the darker colour first. When this is dry, load the stamp with the paler colour and print over the first image, positioning the stamp slightly to one side.

▶

STIPPLED

This stippled effect gives the print lots of surface interest: apply the paint with a stiff brush and a dabbing, stippling motion.

WALLPAPER PASTE

Adding wallpaper paste to emulsion (latex) paint gives the print a translucent, watercolour quality.

LIGHT SHADOW

The paint has been applied with a roller, covering each element of the motif more heavily on one side to create a delicate shadow effect.

SECOND PRINT

After loading the stamp with paint, print first on a piece of scrap paper. This very delicate image is the second print.

SPONGE PRINT

Applying the paint with a sponge gives variable, individual prints.

DISTRESSED

A single colour applied with a dry roller produces an aged, distressed effect.

178

STRAWBERRY FRUIT BASKET

Strawberry motifs always look fresh and pretty, with their bright red fruits and shapely leaves,
and the sponging technique used here suits the texture of strawberries particularly well.
This decorative planter would look lovely on a kitchen windowsill filled with herbs, or, of course,
with strawberry plants.

YOU WILL NEED
medium-grade sandpaper
wooden planter
broad, medium and fine paintbrushes
white matt emulsion (latex) paint
medium-density sponge, such as a kitchen sponge
marker pen
scissors or craft knife and cutting mat
pencil
acrylic paints in red, green and yellow
paint-mixing container
clear acrylic varnish

1 Lightly sand the wooden planter to prepare the surface for painting.

2 Apply two coats of white emulsion paint, allowing the paint to dry and sanding lightly between coats.

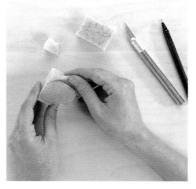

3 Copy the strawberry, leaf and calyx designs from the back of the book. Draw around them on the sponge with a marker pen and cut away the sponge around the shapes using scissors or a craft knife and cutting mat.

4 Mark the positions of the strawberries on the planter. Load the strawberry stamp with red acrylic paint, then stamp the strawberries on the planter. Allow to dry.

▶

179

5 Load the calyx stamp with green acrylic paint and stamp just above the strawberry shapes.

6 Mark the positions of the large and small leaves on the planter. Load the leaf stamp with green paint and stamp the leaves, making the large leaves by stamping three times.

7 Allow the leaves to dry, then use a pencil to mark the positions of the stems and paint them free-hand using a fine paintbrush and green paint.

8 Use a fine paintbrush to paint yellow seeds on the strawberries. When the paint is dry, apply two coats of acrylic varnish to protect the design.

FLOWER-POT FRIEZE

This witty frieze has a 1950s feel and creates an eye-catching feature above a half-boarded wall.
Use scraps of leftover wallpaper or sheets of wrapping paper for the pots, and stamp an exuberant
display of flowers around your kitchen.

YOU WILL NEED
matt emulsion (latex) paints in pale blue and white
broad and fine paintbrushes
old cloth
pencil
wallpaper or wrapping paper
scissors
PVA (white) glue
green acrylic paint
stamp inkpads in a variety of colours
large and small daisy rubber stamps
cotton wool buds (swabs)
scrap paper

1 Paint tongue-and-groove boarding or the lower half of the wall with pale blue emulsion (latex) paint and leave to dry.

2 Using a dry paintbrush, lightly brush white emulsion over the flat colour. For a softer effect, rub the paint in with an old cloth.

3 To make the frieze, draw flower-pot shapes on to scraps of different wallpapers or wrapping papers and cut them out. Cut scalloped strips of paper and glue one along the top of each flower pot, using PVA (white) glue.

4 Glue the flower pots along the wall, at evenly spaced intervals.

5 Using acrylic paint and a fine paintbrush, paint green stems coming out of each pot. Leave the paint to dry before beginning to print the flowers.

6 Use coloured inkpads to ink the daisy stamps, using the lighter colours first. To ink the flower centre in a different colour, remove the first colour from the centre using a cotton wool bud (swab), then use a small inkpad to dab on the second colour.

7 Test the stamp on a sheet of scrap paper before applying it to the wall.

▶

183

8 Print the lighter-coloured flowers on the ends of some of the stems, using large and small daisy stamps. Allow the ink to dry.

9 Print the darker flowers on the remaining stems. Allow the flowers to overlap to create full, blossoming pots.

GRAPE-VINE FRIEZE AND GLASSES

This elegant repeating design is a combination of sponging and freehand painting – practise the strokes on paper before embarking on the wall, and keep your hand relaxed to make confident, sweeping lines. It's perfect for a kitchen or conservatory and is repeated on a set of glasses to carry the theme on to the table.

YOU WILL NEED
medium-density sponge, such as a kitchen sponge
marker pen
small coin
scissors or craft knife and cutting mat
ruler
pencil
acrylic paints in purple and blue
paint-mixing container
medium and fine paintbrushes
glasses
kitchen cloth
ceramic paints in purple and blue

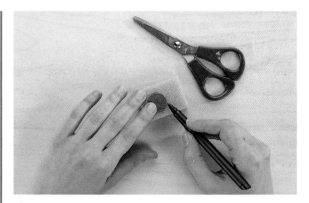

1 Copy the template at the back of the book and use to draw the leaf shape on a piece of medium-density sponge. To make the stamp for the grapes, draw around a coin, or copy the grape template.

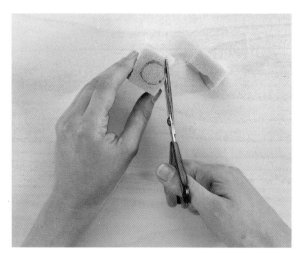

2 Cut out the sponge shapes using a pair of scissors or craft knife.

3 Trace the template of the frieze design on to the wall, carefully marking the positions of the grapes and leaves.

4 Mix up two shades of purple acrylic paint. Using a paintbrush, load one side of the grape stamp with dark purple and the other with a lighter shade to give a shadowed effect.

5 Build up the bunch of grapes, starting with the top row and working downwards to avoid smudges. Position the grapes in succeeding rows diagonally between the ones above. Keep the dark side of each grape facing the same way.

6 Mix up two shades of blue paint and load the leaf stamp, painting the outside edge in the darker shade. Stamp the leaf shape where marked on either side of each bunch of grapes. Paint the stems free-hand in the lighter shade of blue, using a fine brush.

7 Before decorating the glasses with the grape motif, clean each thoroughly to remove any trace of grease. Leave to dry.

▶

8 Mix two shades of purple ceramic paint and load the grape stamp as before. Align the first row of grapes below the edge of the glass, keeping clear of the rim.

9 Build up the bunch of grapes so that it fills one side of the glass.

10 Mix two shades of blue ceramic paint and load the leaf stamp as before. Stamp a leaf motif on either side of the bunch of grapes.

11 Paint the stems in the lighter shade of blue, using a fine brush. Leave the glass for 24 hours to dry completely. The glasses will withstand gentle washing but should not be put in a dishwasher or cleaned with an abrasive scourer.

SPOTTED FLOWER POTS

Customized terracotta pots will give a new, fresh look to your conservatory, patio or kitchen windowsill. Light, bright colours suit this pattern really well, but you can make them as subtle or as bold as you please. The end of a small sponge roller gives a neat, sharp image.

YOU WILL NEED
terracotta flower pots
white acrylic primer
medium paintbrushes
matt emulsion (latex) paints in a variety
of colours including yellow, white, red
and blue
paint-mixing container
old plate
small sponge paint rollers
satin acrylic varnish

1 Make sure the flower pots are clean and dry. Prime them with a coat of white acrylic primer and leave to dry.

2 Dilute some yellow emulsion (latex) paint with water to the consistency of single (light) cream. Colourwash the first pot using a dry brush and random brush strokes. Allow to dry.

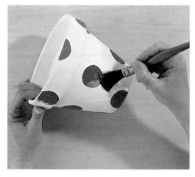

3 Spread some white paint over an old plate. Press the end of a small sponge paint roller into the paint, ensuring that it is totally covered, then press it firmly on to the first flower pot. Remove carefully and repeat all over the pot. Allow to dry.

4 Repeat using red paint over half the white spots, but position the sponge slightly to one side of each white spot to give a highlighted three-dimensional effect. Colour the rest of the spots blue. Leave to dry.

5 Repeat using different colour combinations on the other pots. Seal the pots with 2–3 thin, even coats of satin acrylic varnish, allowing the varnish to dry between coats.

HERB BOX

A miniature chest of drawers with decorations on a botanical theme makes a charming store for dried herbs in the pantry, or would look equally good in the potting shed, filled with seeds. Small, unpainted wooden chests are inexpensive and widely available.

YOU WILL NEED
unpainted wooden chest of drawers
6 unpainted wooden knobs with screws
white acrylic primer
medium paintbrushes
matt emulsion (latex) paints in two shades of pale green
clear wax
medium-grade sandpaper
ruler
pencil
drill and drill bit
rubber stamps in plant designs
green stamp inkpad
screwdriver

1 Prime the chest, drawers and knobs with an even coat of white acrylic primer. Allow to dry. If the drawers have thumb-holes in their fronts, as here, reverse them.

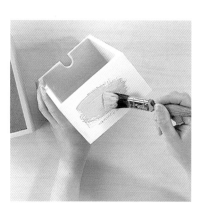

2 Paint the chest, drawers and knobs in pale green and leave to dry thoroughly.

3 Apply clear wax to the edges and corners, wherever the chest and knobs would receive most natural wear and tear. Allow to set for 10 minutes.

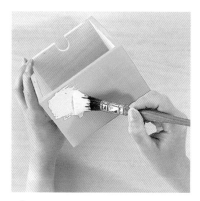

4 Paint on a coat of very pale green and allow to dry.

▶

5 Using medium-grade sandpaper, rub down the areas where the wax was applied to reveal the base colour.

6 Mark each drawer 2.5cm/1in down from the centre top and drill a hole for the knob.

7 Ink a rubber stamp using the inkpad and press on to the drawer below the drilled hole. Choose a different herb or flower design for each drawer.

8 When the stamped designs are dry, screw the knobs to the drawers.

SUN-STAR BLIND

Turn a plain white blind into a chic window dressing by colourwashing it to give a pretty, cloudy effect, then adding a vibrant pattern of stamped motifs. Fix on an ornate blind-pull or tassel to give the finishing touch to the transformation.

YOU WILL NEED

matt emulsion (latex) paints in purple and yellow

acrylic scumble glaze

paint-mixing container

medium paintbrush

plain white roller blind

natural sponge

marker pens in black and gold

paper

scissors

12.5cm/5in square of high density sponge, such as upholstery foam (foam rubber)

craft knife and cutting mat

old plate

bradawl

brass screw eye

blind-pull or tassel

1 Mix some purple emulsion (latex) paint with acrylic scumble glaze. Lay the blind on a flat surface. Dip a natural sponge into the paint and wipe the colour over the blind in a circular motion to give a soft, cloudy effect. Allow to dry.

2 Draw the sun-star design freehand on to a piece of paper and cut it out. Trace around the shape to a square of high-density sponge. Cut out using a craft knife.

3 Spread some yellow emulsion paint over an old plate. Press the sponge on to the paint, making sure the surface is entirely covered, then on to the blind. Repeat, spacing the sun-star evenly and over-lapping the edges of the blind. Allow to dry. ▶

4 Outline each shape and draw in the details using a gold marker pen.

5 Make a hole in the centre of the bottom batten using a bradawl and screw in a small brass eye. Attach a decorative blind-pull or tassel.

MOORISH TILE-EFFECT

Moorish wall patterns are based on abstract, geometric motifs which you can reproduce most effectively with stamps. In this wall treatment, a lozenge shape is incorporated in a subtle tile design on a cool colourwashed background.

YOU WILL NEED

matt emulsion (latex) paints in mid-blue, off-white and terracotta

wallpaper paste

paint-mixing container

broad and fine paintbrushes

thin card (cardboard)

ruler

pencil

scissors

medium-density sponge, such as a kitchen sponge

marker pen

craft knife and cutting mat

spirit level (carpenter's level)

1 Mix the mid-blue emulsion (latex) with 50% wallpaper paste and apply to the walls with a broad brush, working at random angles and blending the brushstrokes to avoid any hard edges.

2 Mix the off-white emulsion with 75% wallpaper paste and brush on to the walls as before, to soften the effect. Allow to dry.

3 To make a template for the tile shape, cut out a 30cm/12in square of thin card (cardboard).

4 Mark the sides of the square 5cm/2in from each corner, draw a line across the diagonal and cut off the corners.

5 Copy the template from the back of the book and transfer it to a 5cm/2in square of medium-density sponge using a marker pen. Cut away the excess sponge using a craft knife.

6 Using a spirit level (carpenter's level), draw a horizontal line around the room where you want the top of the pattern. Place the top of the card template against the line and draw around it. Repeat over the pattern area.

7 Use paintbrushes to load the stamp with mid-blue and terracotta emulsion paint and print the motif in the diamond shapes created by the template.

▶

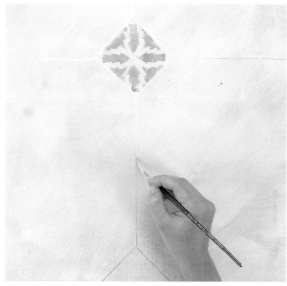

8 Dilute off-white emulsion with enough water to give the consistency of thick cream and use a fine paintbrush to paint over the pencil lines.

SANTA FE LIVING ROOM

Aztec motifs, like this bird, are bold, stylized and one-dimensional, and translate perfectly into stamps. Strong colour contrasts suit this style, but here the pattern is confined to widely spaced stripes over a cool white wall, and further restrained with a final light wash of white paint.

YOU WILL NEED

matt emulsion (latex) paints in off-white, warm white, deep red
and navy blue
paint-mixing container
natural sponge
broad and medium paintbrushes
plumbline
ruler
pencil
masking tape
marker pen
medium-density sponge, such as a household sponge
craft knife and cutting mat
small paint roller
old plate
high-density sponge, such as upholstery foam (foam rubber)

1 Dilute the off-white emulsion (latex) with 50% water and apply a wash over the wall using a sponge, alternating the angle at which you work. Allow to dry.

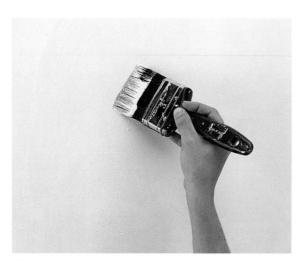

2 Using a broad, dry brush, apply warm white emulsion in some areas of the wall to achieve a rough-looking surface. Allow to dry.

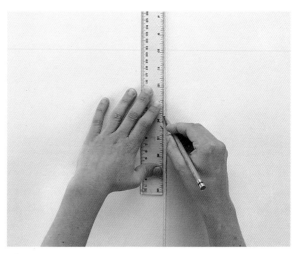

3 Starting 10cm/4in from one corner, and using a plumbline as a guide, draw a straight line from the top to the bottom of the wall.

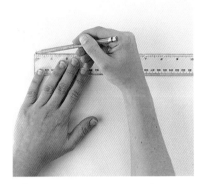

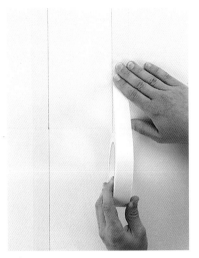

4 Measure 45cm/18in along the wall, hang the plumbline again and mark a second vertical line. Draw another line 10cm/4in away to create a band. Repeat all across the wall.

5 Apply masking tape to the wall on each outer edge of the marked bands.

6 Paint the bands in deep red emulsion. Leave to dry.

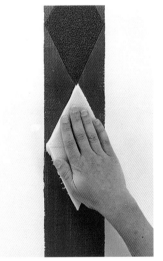

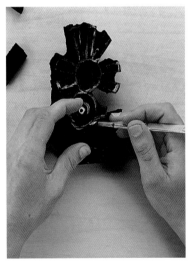

7 Draw a 10 x 20cm/4 x 8in diamond shape on a medium-density sponge and cut out the shape using a craft knife and cutting mat.

8 Use a small roller to load the stamp with navy blue emulsion paint and stamp the diamonds down the red bands, starting from the top and just touching at their tips.

9 Copy the bird template at the back of the book on to a piece of high-density sponge. Cut away the excess sponge using a craft knife.

▶

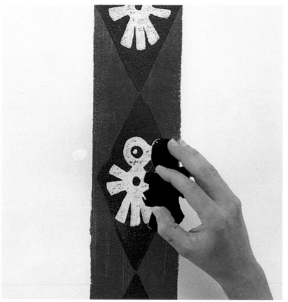

10 Use the roller to load the bird stamp with off-white emulsion and print the birds upright, roughly in the centre of the diamonds.

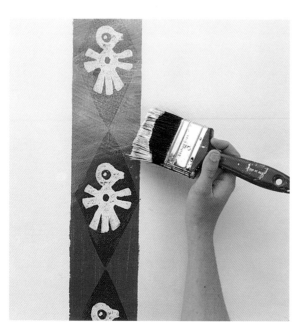

11 When the motifs are dry, use minimal pressure and a dry brush to brush gently over each band with warm white emulsion.

FOLK-ART CHAIR

Simple repeating designs on a white painted chair have a wonderfully naïve charm. Stick to a few bright colours in keeping with the folk-art style of this design, which any slight irregularities in the stamping will only serve to enhance.

YOU WILL NEED
medium-grade sandpaper
wooden chair
white matt emulsion (latex) paint
medium paintbrushes
pencil
scissors
medium-density sponge, such as a kitchen sponge
marker pen
coin
cork from a wine bottle
craft knife and cutting mat
ruler
acrylic paints in black, red, terracotta and blue
paint-mixing container
scrap paper
clear acrylic varnish

1 Sand the chair to remove any rough patches or old paint or varnish.

2 Paint the chair with two coats of white emulsion (latex) paint, allowing the paint to dry between coats.

3 Copy the designs from the back of the book and cut out paper templates of the heart and leaf shapes. Draw around the templates on to the sponge using a marker pen. Draw around a coin on the end of a cork to make the spot stamp.

4 Cut out the excess sponge and cork around the motifs using a craft knife.

▶

207

5 Using a pencil and ruler, mark the positions of the leaves, 6cm/2½in apart, on the struts of the chair back and seat.

6 Load the leaf stamp with black acrylic paint, then stamp once on a piece of scrap paper to remove excess paint. Stamp along the struts at a 45° angle. Alternate the direction of the leaves on each strut.

7 Load the heart stamp with red acrylic paint, remove the excess paint as before and stamp a heart at the top of each vertical strut, across the back and front of the chair.

8 Load the cork with terracotta acrylic paint, remove the excess paint as before and stamp a dot between each leaf shape.

9 Wash the terracotta paint off the cork, load it with blue and stamp dots 2cm/¾in apart along the legs and all round the edge of the chair.

10 Leave the paint to dry, then apply two coats of varnish to protect the design.

STAMPED WRAPPING PAPER

You can turn plain sheets of paper into fabulous hand-printed gift wrap using simple, bold lino-cut motifs and coloured inks. The designs are finished off using small rubber stamps. For the chequerboard design, position the lino block carefully to get an even pattern. Cut up a large sheet to make gift tags, threaded with narrow ribbon.

YOU WILL NEED
linoleum board
marker pen
wood offcut
lino-cutting tools
water-soluble printing ink in a variety of colours
small pane of glass or old saucer
rubber ink roller
wrapping paper
metal spoon
small star and spot rubber stamps
stamp inkpads in a variety of colours

1 Draw the star and star outline freehand onto paper. Cut out and copy on to two squares of lino, using a marker pen.

2 Butt the first lino square against an offcut of wood and place that against a wall on a flat surface, to prevent the lino slipping. Cut away the area around the design using lino–cutting tools.

3 To cut out the spots for the star outline you will need a fine cutting tool. Place the point of the tool on a marked spot and scoop out the lino. Dust away the shavings.

4 Select a coloured ink for the star shape and squeeze a small amount on to a piece of glass or old saucer. Roll out the ink until it feels tacky, then roll it on to the star stamp. Do not apply too much or the lino will slip when printing. ▶

5 Position the star stamp on the paper and press down, holding firmly in place. Smooth the back of the lino with the back of a metal spoon. Reapply the ink before printing each star.

6 Use a darker shade of ink for the star outline and line it up carefully over the plain shape. Smooth over the back with a spoon as before, and print the outline over all the stars.

7 To complete the star design, use a small star-shaped rubber stamp and coloured inkpads to match the large stars. Apply the small stars at random between the large ones.

8 Follow the design in the picture to make a chequerboard stamp in the same way. Finish with a small spot-shaped rubber stamp on each square.

ART NOUVEAU ROSES

This stylized, flowing design is inspired by the rose motif found in the work of Charles Rennie Mackintosh, who used it repeatedly in his interior designs, on chairs, doors, leaded glass and textiles. Used here to link a chair with the wall behind it, it is equally effective as a single motif or as a repeating pattern.

YOU WILL NEED
pencil
scissors
high-density sponge, such as upholstery foam (foam rubber)
craft knife and cutting mat
ruler
stiff card (cardboard)
PVA (white) glue
medium paintbrushes
marker pen
coin
acrylic paints in pink and green
director's chair with calico cover
tailor's chalk
fabric paints in green and pink

1 Scale up the designs at the back of the book to the size you require and make templates. Cut a square of sponge to fit the rose and a rectangle for the stem. Cut two pieces of card (cardboard) to fit the sponge shapes and glue them on.

2 Using a marker pen, transfer the designs to the sponge by drawing around the templates. Mark the top of each design on the card at the back.

3 Cut away the excess sponge from around the motifs using a craft knife. Make the stamp for the small dots by drawing around a coin and cutting out.

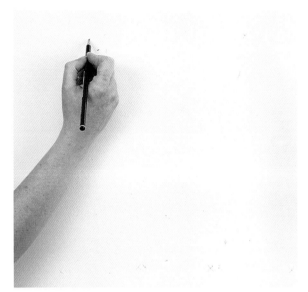

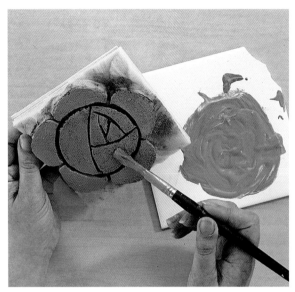

4 Using a pencil and ruler, and with the large stamp as a size guide, mark the positions of the bottom edges of the roses and stems on the wall, keeping the line parallel with the dado rail (chair rail). Repeat for the upper line of roses, then mark the centres of the small dots directly above the lower ones, and on a line equidistant from the two rows of roses.

5 Load the rose stamp with pink acrylic paint.

6 Match the bottom edge of the stamp to the marked wall and apply the stamp.

7 Load the small dot with green acrylic paint and stamp at the marked points.

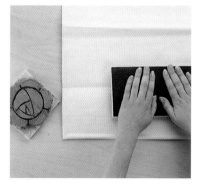

8 Load the stem stamp with green paint and stamp at the marked points. Repeat to complete the rows.

9 Remove the cover from the back of the chair and lay it out flat. Using chalk, mark the positions for the motifs along a line 5cm/2in in from each side. Load the stem stamp with green fabric paint and position the bottom edge on the marked line.

10 Load the rose stamp with pink fabric paint to complete the stamped design. Leave to dry, then rub off the chalk marks and fix the fabric paints according to the manufacturer's instructions.

PLASTER WALL TREATMENT

Add an extra dimension to stamping and create a relief effect on your walls. For this technique, a mixture of paint and interior filler (spackle) is applied to the stamp and then pressed on to the wall, leaving a raised motif. A monochromatic scheme suits this look best.

YOU WILL NEED
matt emulsion (latex) paints in off-white, lime white and
stone white
wallpaper paste
paint-mixing container
broad and medium paintbrushes
45cm/18in square card (cardboard)
pencil
high-density sponge, such as upholstery foam (foam rubber)
marker pen or white crayon
craft knife and cutting mat
interior filler (spackle)

1 Mix the off-white emulsion (latex) with 50% wallpaper paste and apply to the walls with a broad paintbrush, working at random angles and keeping the effect quite rough.

2 Apply random patches of lime white, allowing the basecoat to show in areas.

3 Using the card (cardboard) square as a template and beginning in a corner of the room, make a small mark at each corner of the card. Reposition the card using the previous marks as a guide and repeat to form a grid of evenly spaced marks around the room.

4 Copy the template at the back of the book and transfer it to a piece of high-density sponge. Cut away the excess sponge using a craft knife.

5 Mix stone white emulsion with interior filler (spackle), using about one part filler to three parts paint.

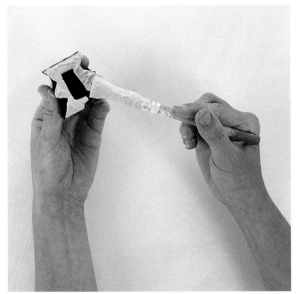

6 Apply the mixture thickly to the stamp using a dabbing motion.

7 Print over each pencil mark, pressing the stamp quite hard and pulling it cleanly away – be careful not to smear the impression. Leave for about 4 hours to dry. ▶

8 Dry brush a little lime white emulsion over each stamp, so that only the areas in highest relief pick up the paint.

GOTHIC DINING ROOM

Create a dramatic setting for candlelit dinner parties with purple and gold panels that will shimmer from deep velvety green walls. The effect is achieved by stamping the wall with gold size and then rubbing on Dutch gold leaf which will adhere to the stamped motifs.

YOU WILL NEED
30cm/12in square thin card
(cardboard)
ruler
pencil
scissors
high-density sponge, such as
upholstery foam (foam rubber)
marker pen
craft knife and cutting mat
matt emulsion (latex) paints in
dark green and purple
natural sponge
plumbline
small paint roller
old plate
gold size
Dutch gold leaf
soft brush

1 To make a template for the wall panels, draw a freehand arc from the centre top of the card (cardboard) square to the lower corner.

2 Fold the card in half down the centre and cut out both sides to make a symmetrical Gothic arch shape.

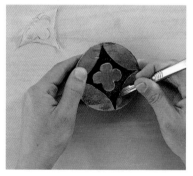

3 Copy the design from the back of the book and make a paper pattern with a diameter of 10cm/4in. Transfer the design on to a piece of high-density sponge. Cut away the excess sponge using a craft knife.

4 Apply dark green emulsion (latex) liberally to the wall, using a sponge and working in a circular motion. Allow to dry.

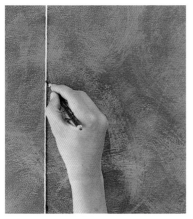

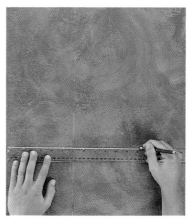

5 Using a plumbline as a guide and beginning 23cm/9in from a corner, mark a vertical line up the wall to a height of 1.8m/6ft.

6 Measure across the wall and use the plumbline to draw vertical lines every 60cm/2ft.

7 Measure out 15cm/6in each side of each vertical and draw two more lines to mark the edges of the panels.

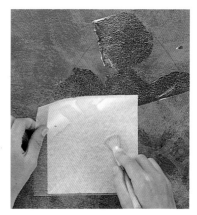

8 Place the point of the card template at the centre top point of each panel and draw in the curves.

9 Use a small paint roller to load the stamp with gold size and print each panel, beginning with the centre top and working down the central line, then down each side.

10 When the size is tacky, apply Dutch gold leaf by rubbing over the backing paper with a soft brush.

▶

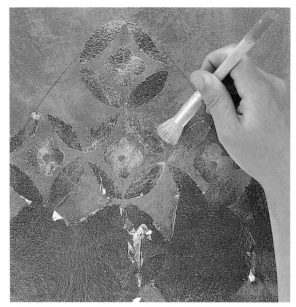

11 Once the panel is complete, use a soft brush to remove any excess gold leaf.

12 Using only the centre of the stamp, fill in the spaces between the gold motifs using purple emulsion paint.

INDIAN VELVET CUSHION

*Indian textile printing blocks are available in numerous designs. This is an opulent way to
decorate cushions or other fabric accessories. Add metallic powders to fabric-painting medium to
give a glittery effect with a hard-wearing finish.*

YOU WILL NEED
150cm/1½yd velvet
tape measure
scissors
dressmaker's pins
sewing machine and matching sewing thread
4 gold tassels
bronze powder
fabric-painting medium
paint-mixing container
medium paintbrush
scrap paper
Indian textile printing block
3 gold buttons
sewing needle
56cm/22in cushion pad

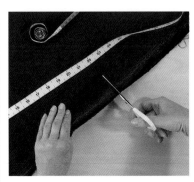

1 Cut out a 58cm/23in square
and two rectangles 33 x 58cm/
13 x 23in from the velvet.

2 To make the back of the
cushion, turn in, pin and
stitch a double hem along one
long edge of each rectangle. Make
three buttonholes, evenly spaced,
in the hem of one piece.

3 Right sides together, pin the
buttonholed piece to the
square front on three sides. Pin
the second back piece on top,
stitched hems overlapping. Insert
a tassel in the seam at each
corner, facing in. Stitch and turn
through. Flatten the seams and lay
the cushion on a flat surface.

4 Add one part bronze powder
to two parts fabric-painting
medium and mix thoroughly.
Insert scrap paper inside the
cushion. Paint an even coat of the
mixture on to the block. Position
the block along one edge of the
cushion and press down firmly.
Repeat to complete the design.

5 Remove the scrap paper. Sew
a gold button opposite each
buttonhole on the back of the
cushion cover. Insert the pad and
fasten the buttons.

SAILING-BOAT FRIEZE

Use this charming yacht bobbing on the waves to complete a bathroom with a nautical theme. It is better, if possible, to stamp tiles before fixing them to the wall, so that the ceramic paints can be made more resilient by baking in the oven. You can stamp and appliqué the same design, with embroidered details, on to your towels.

YOU WILL NEED
high-density sponge, such as
upholstery foam (foam rubber)
craft knife and cutting mat
ruler
stiff card (cardboard)
PVA (white) glue
medium paintbrush
pencil
scissors
marker pen
ceramic paints in
various colours
paint-mixing container

15cm/6in square ceramic tiles
old cloth
methylated spirits (rubbing
alcohol)
plain light-coloured cotton fabric
masking tape
fabric paints
embroidery hoop
stranded embroidery thread
sewing needle
dressmaker's pins
hand towel
8 pearl buttons

1 Cut a 15cm/6in square and a 15 x 5 cm/6 x 2in rectangle of sponge to make the stamps. Cut a piece of card (cardboard) for each square and glue one on to each sponge.

2 Scale up the designs at the back of the book to fit a 15cm/6in tile and make paper templates. Draw around the boat and wave designs on the square stamp using a marker pen.

3 Cut away the excess sponge around the design using a craft knife. Repeat on the rectangular sponge to make the second stamp, positioning the waves so that they will fall between the first set.

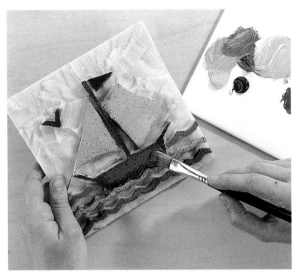

4 Load the boat stamp with ceramic paints, applying the colours to the different areas using a paintbrush.Clean any grease from the surface of the tiles by rubbing with a cloth dipped in methylated spirits (rubbing alcohol). Allow to dry.

5 Press the stamp over the tile. Allow to dry. Load the waves stamp and stamp another set of waves between the first set.

6 For the wave tiles, re-load the wave stamp with paint and position it 1 cm/½ in from the bottom edge. Apply the stamp, aligning it with the bottom edge. Print birds at a 45° angle above the waves.

Above: Using the same design on your tilework and linen adds a pleasing unity to your bathroom's interior design. ▶

7 For the appliqué towel panel, cut out a 17cm/7in square of fabric and tape it to the work surface. Mix fabric paints to match the ceramic paint colours and load the boat motif as before. Stamp on to the fabric and leave to dry.

8 Fix the paints according to the manufacturer's instructions, then insert the panel in an embroidery hoop and work a running stitch to pick out the clouds and details on the sail and boat in stranded embroidery thread.

9 Press under a 1 cm/½ in hem all round the panel and pin it in place at one end of the towel. Work a blanket stitch all round the panel to attach it.

10 Stitch a pearl button to each corner of the panel, and one in the middle of each side.

SCANDINAVIAN BEDROOM

This delicate stamped decoration on walls and woodwork is designed to go with the pale colours and painted furniture that characterize period Scandinavian interiors. This is a scheme of great charm, restful on the eye and perfect for a bedroom.

YOU WILL NEED
matt emulsion (latex) paints in grey blue, off-white and red
paint-mixing container
wallpaper paste
broad and fine paintbrushes
plumbline
ruler
pencil
marker pen or white crayon
high-density sponge, such as upholstery foam (foam rubber)
craft knife and cutting mat
small paint roller
old plate
matt acrylic varnish

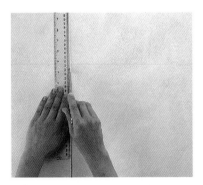

1 Mix the grey-blue emulsion (latex) with 50% wallpaper paste and apply to the walls with a broad paintbrush, working at random angles and blending the brushstrokes to avoid hard edges.

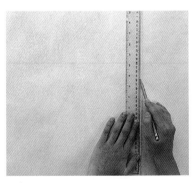

2 Allow to dry, then repeat the process to soften the effect.

3 Mix the off-white emulsion with 75% wallpaper paste and brush on to the walls as before. Allow to dry.

4 Hang a plumbline 2.5cm/1in from one corner and use as a guide to draw a vertical line down the wall.

5 Measure about 40cm/16in across and draw a second vertical line, again using the plumbline as a guide. Repeat all around the room.

6 Scale up the template at the back of the book and draw it on a rectangle of high-density sponge. Cut away the excess sponge around the design using a craft knife.

7 Use a small paint roller to load the stamp with off-white emulsion paint.

8 Add details in red and grey-blue emulsion, using a paint-brush to add the colours over the off-white paint.

9 Apply the stamp to the wall, positioning it centrally over the marked line.

10 Repeat, positioning the stamp so that each motif is just touching the preceding one. Work down from the top of the wall.

11 Use the grey-blue wash mixed for the wall basecoat to drag the door: applying pressure to the bristles, pull down in a straight line, following the direction of the wood grain.

▶

12 Apply the paint to the stamp as before, but this time loading only one flower motif. Stamp a single motif diagonally into the corners of each door panel.

13 Add more paint to the grey-blue wash to deepen the colour and use it to edge the door panels. Leave to dry, then apply two coats of matt varnish to the door to protect the design.

ANIMAL FRIEZE

A low frieze is perfect for a nursery as it concentrates interest at the child's own level. Children can't fail to be enchanted by this harmonious troop of animals all sharing the same flowery field, with clouds billowing overhead.

YOU WILL NEED
emulsion (latex) paints in sky blue, grass green, yellow and white
paint roller
broad and fine paintbrushes
paint-mixing container
stamp inkpads in a variety of colours
rubber stamps in cow, chicken, pig and sheep designs
natural sponge

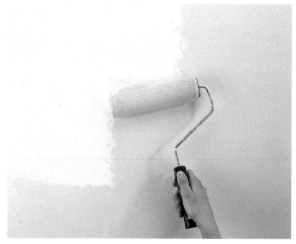

1 Paint the wall in sky blue emulsion (latex) and allow to dry.

2 Paint the skirting-board (baseboard) in a grass green.

3 Using the same green paint, apply wispy strokes up the wall to create the effect of grass. Allow the paint to dry.

4 Using a finer paintbrush, highlight the grass with a lighter, yellowy green.

5 Paint small daisies in white emulsion at random in the grass. Add yellow centres.

6 Using a black inkpad, stamp the cow at random along the frieze.

7 Print groups of chickens, using brown ink.

8 Print the pig, using pink ink.

▶

9 Print the sheep, using black ink. Using a fine paintbrush, fill in the body of the sheep in white emulsion paint. Do the same with the cow if you wish.

10 Lightly press a natural sponge into white emulsion paint and sponge cloud shapes on the sky blue wall above the frieze.

STARRY CABINET

Turn a small junk-shop find into a unique bedside cabinet using a palette of fresh colours and a simple star motif. Before you start to paint, divide the piece visually into blocks, each of which will be a different colour, with a further shade for the frame. Keep all the colours in similar tones to achieve this pretty, sugared-almond effect.

YOU WILL NEED
medium-grade sandpaper
wooden cabinet
wood filler
acrylic wood primer
medium and fine paintbrushes
emulsion (latex) paints in green, pink, blue and yellow
wooden knobs
star rubber stamp
stamp inkpads in a variety of colours
drill and drill bit
screwdriver and screws
masking tape
acrylic spray varnish

1 Sand the cabinet to remove any rough patches or old paint or varnish. Fill any holes with wood filler and sand down. Paint the wood with a coat of primer and leave to dry.

2 Paint the cabinet using different coloured emulsion (latex) paints and allow to dry.

3 Using an assortment of all the colours except that of the frame, paint a row of spots around the frame. ▶

4 Paint the wooden knobs and, when the paint has dried, stamp a contrasting star motif on each one using coloured inkpads. When dry, drill screw holes and screw the knobs into position.

5 Stamp a contrasting star motif on to each of the spots around the cabinet frame.

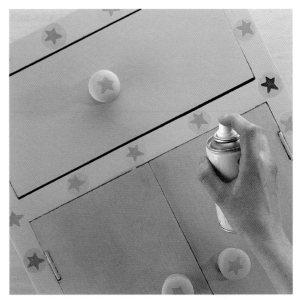

6 Use masking tape to mark out a row of stripes along the bottom of the cabinet and paint them in a contrasting colour.

7 When all the paint is dry, protect it with a coat of acrylic spray varnish. Leave to dry thoroughly.

PAINT TEMPLATES

HARLEQUIN SCREEN

Diagrams to show how to mark
the panels and apply the masking
tape for the project on pages 68–71.

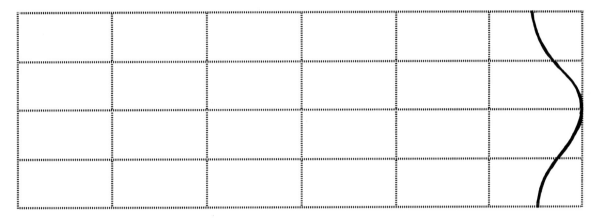

The pencil marks

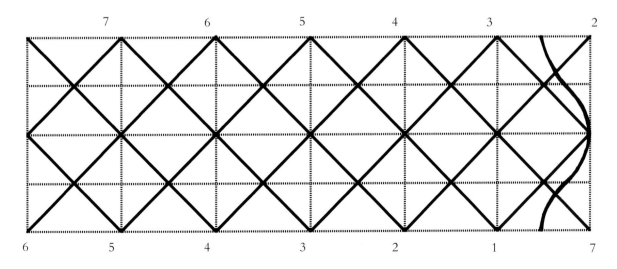

The tape marks

STENCILLING TEMPLATES

Enlarge the templates on a photocopier, or trace the design and draw a grid of evenly spaced squares over your tracing. Draw a larger grid on to another piece of paper and copy the outline square by square. Draw over the lines to make sure they are continuous.

Frosted Vases, pp 99–101. Scale up.

Art Nouveau Hatbox
pp 102–104.
Scale up.

Star Picture Frames
pp 105–107.
Same size.

Making Sandcastles
pp 108–111.
Scale up.

Seashore Bathroom Set pp 112–114.
Same size.

Greek Urns pp 115–117. Same size.

French Country
Kitchen pp 122–125.
Same size.

Tray of Autumn
Leaves pp 126–128.
Same size.

Pennsylvania-Dutch Tulips
pp 118–121. Same size.

Gilded Candles pp 129–131.
Same size.

Renaissance
Art pp 132–135.
Scale up.

Heraldic Dining
Room pp 154–157.
Scale up.

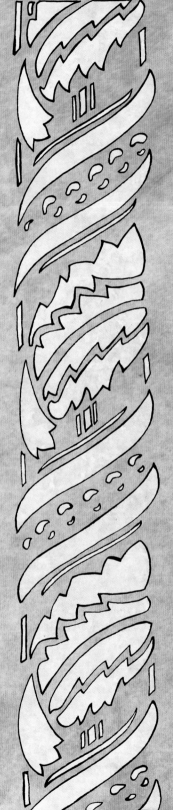

Organza
Cushion
pp 140–142.
Scale up.

Geometric
Floor Tiles
pp 136–139.
Scale up.

*Tablecloth
and Napkins
pp 143–145.
Scale up.*

*Through the
Grapevine
pp 146–149.*

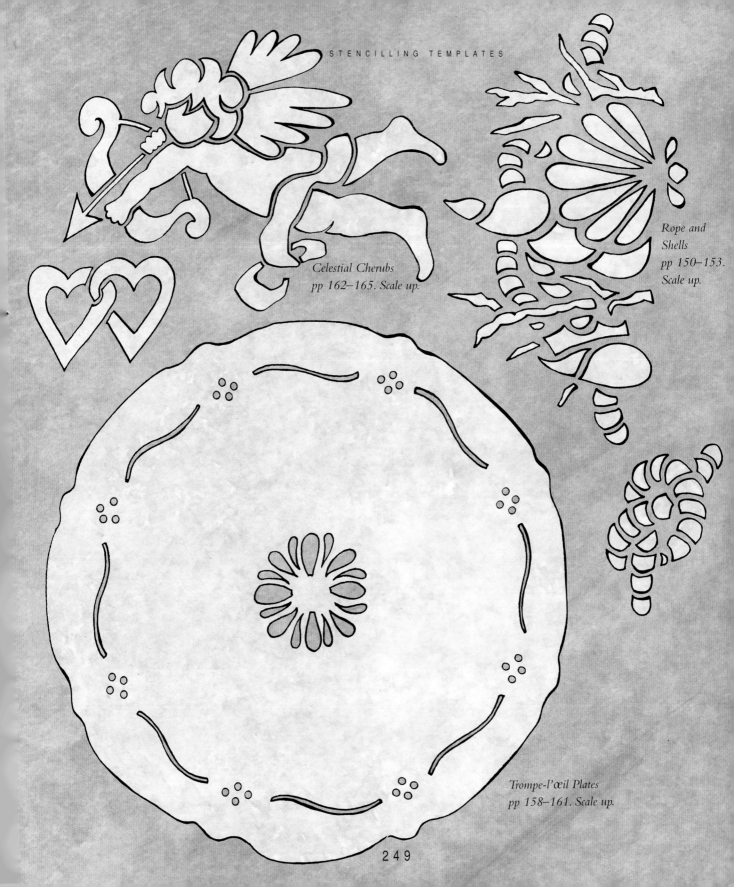

Celestial Cherubs
pp 162–165. Scale up.

Rope and
Shells
pp 150–153.
Scale up.

Trompe-l'œil Plates
pp 158–161. Scale up.

STAMPING TEMPLATES

Enlarge the templates on a photocopier, or trace the design and draw a grid of evenly spaced squares over your tracing. Draw a larger grid on to another piece of paper and copy the outline square by square. Draw over the lines to make sure they are continuous.

Sante Fe Living Room pp 202–205

Gothic Dining Room pp 220–223

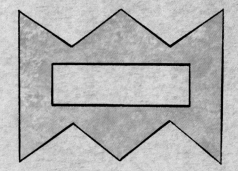

Plaster Wall Treatment pp 216–219

Moorish Tile-effect pp 198–201

Folk-art Chair pp 206–208

Scandinavian Bedroom pp 230–233

Grape-vine Frieze and Glasses pp 186–189

Strawberry Fruit Basket pp 179–181

Art Nouveau Roses pp 212–215

Sailing-boat Frieze
pp 226–229

SUPPLIERS

The materials and equipment for the projects in this book are available from good art supply shops.

UNITED KINGDOM
Cornelissen & Sons Ltd.
105 Great Russell Street
London WC1B 3RY

Crown Paints
Crown Decorative Products Ltd.
PO Box 37
Crown House
Hollins Road
Darwen
Lancashire BB3 0BG

Daler-Rowney Ltd.
PO Box 10
Southern Industrial Estate
Bracknell
Berkshire RG12 8ST

Green and Stone
259 Kings Road
London SW3 5EL

W. Habberley Medows Ltd.
5 Saxon Way
Chelmsley Wood
Birmingham B37 5AY

London Graphic Centre
16 Shelton Street
London WC2H 9JJ
Specialist art supplies

Paint Magic
79 Shepperton Road
Islington
London N1 3DF

Paint Service Co. Ltd.
19 Eccleston Street
London SW1W 9LX

UNITED STATES
Dick Blick
P.O. Box 1267
Galesburg, IL 61402
Tel: (800) 828-4548

Gail Grisi Stenciling Inc.
P.O. Box 1263
Haddonfield, NJ 08033
Tel: (609) 354-1757
Fax: (609) 354-8380

Nasco Arts and Crafts
901 Janesville Avenue
Fort Atkinson, WI 53538
Tel: (800) 558-9595
Fax: (920) 563-8296

Nova Color Artists
Acrylic Paint
5894 Blackwelder Street
Culver City, CA 90232
Tel: (310) 204-6900
www.novacolorpaint.com

Stencil House of New
Hampshire, Inc.
P.O. Box 16109
Hooksett, NH 03106
Tel: (800) 622-9416
Fax: (603) 627-0749

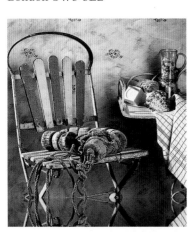

INDEX

This index covers general techniques, materials and equipment. A detailed list of the projects can be found at the front of the book.

ACKNOWLEDGMENTS

The publishers and authors would like to thank the following people for contributing projects to this book:

Petra Boase for the Frosted Vases pp 99–101, Star Frame pp 105–107, Making Sandcastles pp 108–111, Seashore Bathroom Set pp 112–114, Tablecloth and Napkins pp 143–145, Flower Pot Frieze pp 182–185, Animal Frieze pp 234–237, Starry Cabinet pp 238–240 and Stamped Wrapping Paper pp 209–211

Sacha Cohen for the Two-Tone Rollered Wall pp 37–39, Distressed Tabletop pp 60–62, Dry-Brushed Chair pp 63–65, Grained Door pp 66–67, Greek Urns pp 115–117, Through the Grapevine pp 146–149, Rope and Shells pp 150–153, Heraldic Dining Room pp 154–157, Moorish Tile Effect pp 198–201, Santa Fe Living Room pp 202–205, Plaster Wall Treatment pp 216–219, Gothic Dining Room pp 220–223 and Scandinavian Bedroom pp 230–233

Lucinda Ganderton for the Sponged Lamp Base pp 78–81, Crackle-Glaze Planter pp 82–83, Scandinavian Table pp 84–87, Art Nouveau Hatbox pp 102–104, Pennsylvania Dutch Tulips pp 118–121, French Country Kitchen pp 122–125, Renaissance Art pp 132–135, Geometric Floor Tiles pp 136–139, Celestial Cherubs pp 162–165, Grape-Vine Frieze and Glasses pp 186–189, Strawberry Fruit Basket pp 179–181, Folk Art Chair pp 206–208, Art Nouveau Roses pp 212–215 and Sailing-Boat Frieze pp 226–229

Elaine Green for the Vinegar-Glazed Floorcloth pp 53–55, Harlequin Screen pp 68–71 and Grained Window Frame pp 72–73

Emma Hardy for the Tray of Autumn Leaves pp 126–128, Gilded Candles pp 129–131, Organza Cushion pp 140–142 and Trompe l'Oeil Plates pp 158–161

Dinah Kelly for the Combed Checked Floor pp 56–59 and Crackle-Glaze Picture Frame pp 74–77

Liz Wagstaff for the Diamond-Stencilled Wall pp 22–24, Limewashed Wall pp 25–27, Fresco Effect pp 28–29, Stone Wall pp 40–43, Wax-Resist Shutters pp 44–46, Spotted Flower Pots pp 190–191, Herb Box pp 192–194, Sun-Star Blind pp 195–197 and Indian Velvet Cushion pp 224–225

The publishers would like to thank Lizzie Orme and Adrian Taylor for photographing the following projects:

Lizzie Orme for the Grape-Vine Frieze and Glasses p1; Flower Pot Frieze p4; Herb Box p6 t; Gothic Dining Room p166; Santa Fe Living Room p167 bl and top (cl); Spotted Flower Pots p167 br and tr; Flower Pot Frieze p167 tl; Grape-Vine Frieze and Glasses p167 top (cr); Strawberry Fruit Basket pp 179–181; Flower Pot Frieze pp 182–185; Grape-Vine Frieze and Glasses pp 186–189; Spotted Flower Pots pp 190–191; Herb Box pp 192–194; Sun-Star Blind pp 195–197; Moorish Tile Effect pp 198–201; Santa Fe Living Room pp 202–205; Folk Art Chair pp 206–208; Stamped Wrapping Paper pp 209–211; Art Nouveau Roses pp 212–215; Plaster Wall Treatment pp 216–219; Gothic Dining Room pp 220–223; Indian Velvet Cushion pp 224–225; Sailing Boat Frieze pp 226–229; Scandinavian Bedroom pp 230–233; Animal Frieze pp 234–237; Starry Cabinet pp 238–240; Folk Art Chair p254 br; Strawberry Fruit Basket p255 bl

Adrian Taylor for the Grained Window Frame p2; Heraldic Dining Room p3; Gilded Candles p5 tc; French Country Kitchen p5 bc; Dry-Brushed Chair p6 b; Greek Urns p7 bl; Frottage Hallway p7 br; Misty Lilac Stripes p8; Red-Panelled Wall p9 bl; Two-Tone Rollered Wall p9 br, tl and top (cl); Frottage Hallway p9 top (cr); Grained Window Frame p9 tr; Rough Plaster Colourwash pp 20–21; Diamond Stencilled Wall pp 22–24; Limewashed Wall pp 25–27; Fresco Effect pp 28–29; Misty Lilac Stripes pp 30–33; Red-Panelled Wall pp 34–36; Two-Tone Rollered Wall pp 37–39; Stone Wall pp 40–43; Wax-Resist Shutters pp 44–46; Kitchen Tiles pp 47–49; Frottage Hallway pp 50–52; Vinegar-Glazed Floorcloth pp 53–55; Combed Check Floor pp 56–59; Distressed Tabletop pp 60–62; Dry-Brushed Chair pp 63–65; Grained Door pp 66–67; Harlequin Screen pp 68–71; Grained Window Frame pp 72–73; Crackle-Glaze Picture Frame pp 74–77; Sponged Lamp Base pp 78–81; Crackle-Glaze Planter pp 82–83; Scandinavian Table pp 84–87; Pennsylvania Dutch Tulips p88; Celestial Cherubs p89 bl and tl; Renaissance Art p89 top (cl); Art Nouveau Hatbox p89 br and top (cr); Heraldic Dining Room p89 (tr); Frosted Vases pp 99–101; Art Nouveau Hatbox pp 102–104; Star Frame pp 105–107; Making Sandcastles pp 108–111; Seashore Bathroom Set pp 112–114; Greek Urns pp 115–117; Pennsylvania Dutch Tulips pp 118–121; French Country Kitchen pp 122–125; Tray of Autumn Leaves pp 126–128; Gilded Candles pp 129–131; Renaissance Art pp 132–135; Geometric Floor Tiles pp 136–139; Organza Cushion pp 140–142; Tablecloth and Napkins pp 143–145; Through the Grapevine pp 146–149; Rope and Shells pp 150–153; Heraldic Dining Room pp 154–157; Trompe L'Oeil Plates pp 158–161; Celestial Cherubs pp 162–165; Kitchen Tiles p254t; Rope and Shells p254 bl; Limewashed Wall p255 t; Tray of Autumn Leaves p255 br

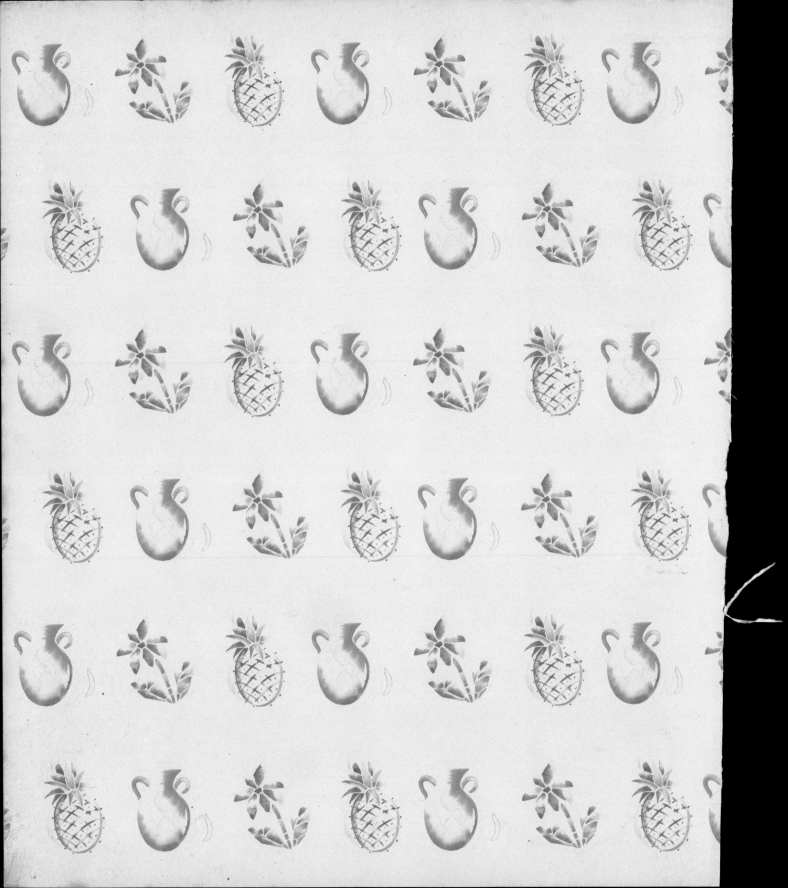